Refugee
for Life

Refugee for Life

My Journey across Africa To Find a Place Called Home

INNOCENT MAGAMBI

with DAVID AEILTS

Cover and Interior Design by AuthorSupport.com

Edit by Grace Smith

Maps by Aly Englund

Printed in the United States of America

ISBN 978-0-9887356-3-7

Library of Congress Control Number 2015939528

Published by:

International Association for Refugees
P.O. Box 47947
Minneapolis, MN 55447
info@iafr.org

Author's Disclaimer: I've tried hard to glean dates and times from family and friends, but few written records survive my early years. I can say two things with certainty: 1) the chronology of this book is only as good as the memory of the witnesses, and 2) the truth of this book does not rest on the accuracy of all dates herein.

TABLE OF CONTENTS

FOREWORD

Every day we hear news bulletins about conflict, about the plight of people who have been caught up in somebody else's war. We see pictures of lorries struggling to move with people who are leaving their town, now devastated by bombs and shells. We hear of people leaving what once was their own village. We hear of people having to move to possible safety in another place.

These people leave their fractured society. They turn their backs on yet another pitiless tyrant. They are the refugees of today who add yet another bleak metric to the mountain of data about people who have lost home, family, identity and hope – twenty-first century refugees.

This book is written by one of them. It gets into the mind of the refugee. It gives no easy simplified prescriptions about what to do, no easy answer to the moral choices which confront any refugee who is running a race to survive. Innocent Magambi spent twenty-seven years as a refugee in five settlements and camps in four African countries. His account of his life does not gloss over difficulties and is tellingly honest about how, as a refugee, he had to deceive to survive. He clearly acknowledges the important work of the Office of the United Nations High Commissioner for Refugees in its all-round advocacy and authority. He now writes from Malawi and the settlement where twenty thousand refugees from African countries live as a large community.

Innocent has written an important book. Not only does he explode common myths about how a refugee community may live, about the extraordinary resilience of people who determine to overcome dreadful difficulties. He also tells the sad truth that animosity between different groups before they are displaced does not go away in a refugee settlement. If his book did no more than dispel myths about refugees, and if it did no more than describe his refugee life, it would be a real help to all those engaged in the support of a refugee community, but it does much more.

Here also is Innocent's own journey of faith, the faith which now governs his life and which he shares with his wife, tested to a tragic limit when their first baby girl, born with significant developmental defects, died despite massive medical care and dedication.

The Magambis are determined to give hope and a future to refugees, to train people out of dependency, to equip young people with skills, and to bring precious hope to a dispossessed community. Their vision is now being realised through There is Hope, an organisation which has developed all sorts of initiatives such as microfinance loans for women or scholarships for vocational and university training. With their team, they are helping to bring self-sufficiency, confidence, and self-respect to some of this world's most forgotten people. It is an inspiration to read.

Sir Eldryd Hugh Owen Parry
Welsh scholar, medical doctor
Author, *Principles of Medicine in Africa*
Founder, Tropical Health and Education Trust

INTRODUCTION

My Oath under Fire

Crack! Crack! Crack! I woke with a start in the early hours of Wednesday morning, April 13, 1994, to the sound of nearby gunfire. I remember the terror of that moment as though it were yesterday.

It was market day in Gitaza, my family's home village on the eastern shore of Lake Tanganyika in the small East African nation of Burundi. Though it was still dark, neighbors who worked as vendors in the marketplace were frying *mandazi*, a deep-fried pastry made of flour, salt and sugar—like the western donut only small and round. The delicious smell wafted through my family's compound, in sharp contrast to the fear now rising in my throat.

Crack! Crack! Crack! My thirteen-year-old body shook violently at the sound of gunfire, and for a moment my mind froze. What should I do?

My sister-in-law's voice from another room propelled me to action. "Innocent!" she commanded. "Wake up the houseboy and tell him to lock the main gate."

I opened the door and crossed the outdoor kitchen to a house opposite. I had to bang hard on the door to wake the young man our family employed to help with household duties. He slept deeply and did not hear the gunfire.

While he and my sister-in-law locked the house and the main gate, I made a decision. I had heard too many accounts of people being burned alive in their houses. I had to leave.

There was no time to dress. Wearing only my shorts, I grabbed my flip-flops and T-shirt and began running toward the mountains.

By that time the shooting had stopped, and I had no idea whether I was running in the right direction. I prayed to God, asking for his protection. It was out of obedience to my father that I had returned to Burundi within months of President Ndadaye's assassination. The killing of our country's newly elected leader had triggered widespread massacres and other acts of violence throughout my country.

My heart pounded in my chest. I was keenly aware of my mortal danger. As I ran, I confessed all my known sins, plus any I might have committed without being aware.

Suddenly, from the top of the mountain, I heard a commanding voice. *Hagarara! Ntunyugange.* "Stop! Don't move." The voice, speaking in my native Kirundi language, came from a spot ten meters distant. Upon hearing this order, I remember pleading, "God receive my heart."

Then I heard the sound of steps in my direction. I shook uncontrollably.

A few seconds later, a man in uniform, carrying a gun, emerged from the bush. He commanded me to put aside whatever I had in my hands and to lie flat. I let go of my T-shirt and shoes, and with my knees buckling under me, I lunged forward to hug the ground.

At that moment, I truly believed my life was over. But after being held captive by soldiers of the Burundian army for several hours, I was released. Not everyone was as fortunate that early Wednesday morning. A boy who attended my primary school had not stopped as commanded, and the soldiers shot him dead.

Even after they released me, I was certain the soldiers would shoot me in the back. I kept looking over my shoulder until I could not see them anymore. My heart was racing as I ran down the mountain, and I praised God for saving me from death.

Then and there, I promised that the whole world would learn of my miraculous escape. This book is a fulfillment of that promise.

Innocent Magambi

PROLOGUE

Origins of Conflict

With topographical features ranging from plains to highlands and mountains, the densely populated inland nation of Burundi ranks among the poorest in the world.

The World Bank estimates Burundi's population at 10.6 million and its gross national income at US$260 per person.

Ninety percent of the nation's population derives all or part of its living from farming. Most citizens grow subsistence crops like corn, sorghum, sweet potatoes, bananas, and cassava. Burundi exports only a handful of its agricultural commodities, the most important being coffee and tea.

The inhabitants of this tiny country belong largely to two people groups or tribes. About 85 percent of the population is Hutu and about

15 percent is Tutsi. A third group, the Twa, make up less than 1 percent of the population.

The two main tribes share similar culture, history, and language. Intermarriage is common, and it is difficult to distinguish a Hutu from a Tutsi. Historically, Hutu names had to do with God or with a life of struggle. Tutsi names had to do with beauty, fighting, and cattle—since they were herders. In recent years, this has changed. The use of names is more fluid between tribes. Regardless of appearance or name, tribal affiliation is inherited from the father.

One of Africa's smallest nations, Burundi had its origins in the 1400s when Tutsi settlers arrived in this region where Hutus had already settled. In the 1500s, a distinct kingdom, Urundi, emerged in the approximate geographical area that is now Burundi. The royal caste, Baganwa, was placed above both Hutus and Tutsis and claimed to have mixed ancestry. In general, Tutsi held the higher rank in society, although some Hutus played administrative roles. For centuries, this arrangement functioned in a relatively stable fashion.

Germany colonized present-day Burundi in the 1800s. After Germany lost World War I, Belgium gained control of Burundi. Both world powers ruled through the traditional kingship, but the Belgians instituted a more rigid class hierarchy that favored the Tutsi and forced the Hutu into positions of subservience. This artificial hierarchy, originally intended to prevent the dissent of the majority, would lead to persistent strife between the two tribes during and after Burundians gained their independence from Belgium in the 1960s.

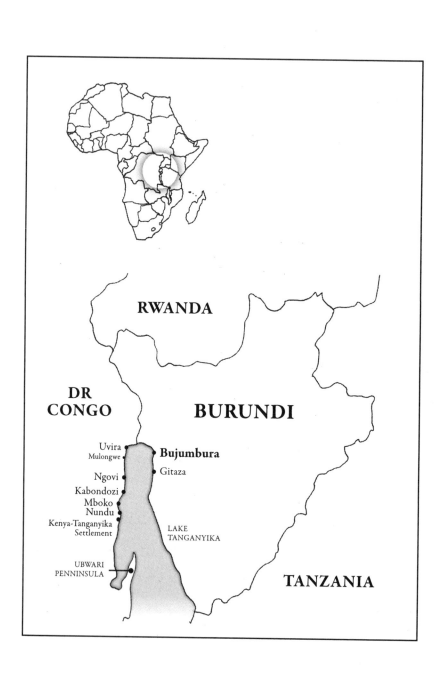

CHAPTER 1

A Heritage of Homelessness

*I*t is sad to come from a country where you could never live—a country *of which you have no memory—all because of hatred between brothers. So it was in my native Burundi where my story begins even before my birth.*

The Burundian dilemma began years ago, after my country's independence in 1964 from Belgium. Instead of enjoying our freedom and working together in the interest of community and country, our leaders nurtured the same toxic seed of tribal hatred that colonial rulers had planted among Hutus and Tutsis as a divide and conquer strategy. Consequently, thousands of Burundians of both tribes died at each other's hands. This is a part of my heritage of which I am deeply ashamed. Another part of my heritage is my father and my family—of which I am, for the most part, very proud. You will meet them in this book.

My story is pieced together from my earliest memories, as well as from present-day conversations with family members and friends. I have tried to be as accurate as possible with regard to the facts, while taking into account the feelings of the times. I apologize for any misrepresentation.

A BUSINESSMAN OF VISION

My father, Meshack Surwavuba, was a man whose character and vision was much bigger than his physical appearance. An ordinary looking Burundian, not tall and not fat, Dad's most memorable trait was his business acumen. He had an innate ability to relate to people.

For example, Dad would purchase coffee beans from farmers in the highlands and resell them in the coastal markets. When he traveled to the mountains, Dad would join the farmers in their manual labor, chatting amicably for many minutes before asking if they had coffee beans for sale. Because of his humility and friendliness, farmers would go out of their way to do business with Dad—to the point of selling him coffee they were keeping for other clients.

Dad taught his children some important lessons as we watched the way he treated other people. A successful businessman with many people working for him, Dad taught us to treat employees as peers. Although they received a fair wage at the end of the day, Dad allowed them to share in our lunch and even helped them with their work.

He also taught us not to pass by women or children carrying heavy loads. If they showed signs of tiredness, Dad would insist we stop and carry their load for a while—something that was beyond the call of duty even by traditional social customs. Occasionally, he would even ask us to help someone walking in the opposite direction from where we were going.

As a child, I found the thought of helping strangers annoying. "It is none of our business," I protested, when in fact I objected to getting sweaty and dirty carrying things on my head. Today, I appreciate my dad's teachings. They've made me a community-oriented person, able to look beyond my personal needs.

Dad loved to whistle whole songs, especially hymns. Whenever he was going somewhere by foot or bicycle, he would whistle away. We could always tell he was coming home as we could hear him whistling in the distance.

Although uneducated, my father learned to make money at a young age by following the example of his elder brother Marwandi. A man of trustworthy character, Marwandi knew how to attract the favor of people. He also knew how to open doors by creating a good rapport with authorities.

Following the model of his brother, Dad became a successful businessman in the province of Bujumbura Rural and the district of Muhuta, where Gitaza is located. He was the first to open a fueling station in Gitaza, using barrels of petrol and manual pumps. He had three motorboats for fishing, numerous bars and shops, and farms where he grew crops and raised animals for meat. Dad owned a compound in the capital city of Bujumbura, about 30 kilometers (19 miles) north of Gitaza, and many other houses and lands. But his major trade was coffee. He hired workers to carry coffee on their heads from Gitaza to Bujumbura, and when trucks became more common in Burundi, he hired them to transport his goods. My father, Meshack Surwavuba, achieved all this before the killings began.

THE 1972 KILLINGS

In April of 1972, a small rural Hutu-led rebellion resulted in the killing of hundreds of military and government officials, as well as a number of Tutsi citizens. The poorly equipped rebellion was quickly squelched by the well-armed forces of the Tutsi-dominated government. But the killing didn't stop there. The military's response to this rebellion quickly turned into a national bloodletting in which tens of thousands died.

Most victims of the post-rebellion violence were civilians, and the overwhelming majority was Hutu with education or wealth. Estimates of those killed range from 150,000 to 300,000 people in a nation with a population of about four million people in 1972. If 200,000 people were killed, then one in twenty people lost their lives.

Not all victims were Hutu, and not all Tutsis participated in or consented to what has been variously called genocide, ethnic cleansing, or nationalism run amuck. But Tutsis had full control of the armed forces which, along with the ruling party's militant youth wing, the *Jeunesses Révolutionnaires Rwagasore* (JRR), local officials and some ordinary citizens, stand accused of inciting and engaging in the majority of the violence.

Witnesses estimate 20,000 people died in the Muhuta District, my family's home.

A FRIEND TURNED FOE

As an entrepreneur and a Hutu, my father had strong relationships with both Hutus and Tutsis in positions of leadership. This assured him of success in his business dealings.

When the killings began, Dad never dreamed he would be affected. He had confidence in his friend, Mr. Joseph Rudigi, a Tutsi and the administrator of the Muhuta District. He soon discovered, however, that Mr. Rudigi was not to be trusted.

Survivors tell of Mr. Rudigi sending agents of the JRR to gather and then murder Hutu businessmen, government and religious leaders, teachers, students— all who had wealth or influence in the community.

According to one account, Mr. Rudigi gave the JRR a list of people to be called to a mandatory meeting chaired by himself. When the people arrived, they were surrounded by police who beat them with hammers and hoes until they were dead. Others testify that Mr. Rudigi called people to answer legal charges, and they never returned. Still others were invited for a drink, never to be seen again.

At one point in the killings, Mr. Rudigi paid a visit to my family's house in Bujumbura. He seemed startled to see Dad there and was most likely surprised to see him still alive. After a brief conversation, Mr. Rudigi invited Dad to meet him at his office in Gitaza. As my father prepared to go, friends told him of the killings taking place throughout the district. They urged him not to go, but Dad found these reports hard to believe, so he went anyway—using a different route than usual.

Approaching Mr. Rudigi's office, Dad witnessed someone being killed in the nearby bush. Immediately, he turned and fled to the mountains.

LEAVING EMPTY-HANDED

In the mountains, Dad was surrounded by people who loved him. Members of the Hutu resistance lived in the hidden places of the hills.

Some had been Dad's employees. Some were family members and friends.

A few days after Dad's flight, Mr. Rudigi sent an army officer named Bunori along with two policemen to search for those on his list who had escaped capture and execution. The Hutu resistance caught and killed the two policemen, but Bunori escaped—creating the very real risk that those in hiding would be hunted down and killed. The danger was so great that Dad and many other prominent Hutus became convinced their only chance to survive was to flee Burundi and seek asylum in another country.

> *For more insight to the 1972 Hutu exodus from Burundi, read "A Meeting of Survivors" on page 147.*

Those circumstances led Dad to step into a crowded fishing boat and cross Lake Tanganyika to Zaire—the present-day Democratic Republic of Congo.[1] With him was his second wife Guenèse, who would become my mother, and two sons: Harimbabazi (Hari), their eldest child, and Nkeshimana (Josaphat), their second born.[2]

My father later told me, "I had to struggle with an old proverb that said 'only those too poor to afford the colonial tax owed by all adult male Burundians would stoop to the level of

> *Learn the difference between a refugee and migrant. Read "Running for His Life" on page 153.*

---

1   To avoid confusion, I will refer to my father's country of refuge as Congo from this point forward.

2   Polygamy was a sign of wealth. My father had two wives, but only my mother-to-be fled with him to Congo.

living in Congo.'" It had been almost eighteen years since the Belgians left Burundi, but that belief was still strong in my father's mind as he crossed the lake into exile.

A well-to-do businessman on the opposite shore, Dad stepped out of the boat onto Congolese soil, a refugee with empty hands.

CHAPTER 2

Born a Refugee

The 1972 killings drove an estimated 150,000 Burundians to the neighboring countries of Rwanda, Tanzania, and Congo. The largest number fled to Tanzania. Living close to Lake Tanganyika, my family crossed over with their neighbors by boat to Congo.

The prospect of certain death if they chose to stay forced thousands to make this heart-wrenching journey. Traumatized by the blood being spilled across their beloved nation and with no time to prepare, husbands abandoned wives and children. Sons and daughters deserted aging parents. Farmers left crops in the field and animals in pens. Eyewitnesses report that up to ten grief-stricken people crammed into each two-man fishing boat for the five-to-eight-hour crossing of Lake Tanganyika.

The fleeing Burundians carried few personal possessions due to the suddenness of their departure and the limited space. War also ravaged their country of refuge, and rebels often confiscated the Burundians' meager belongings after they landed in Congo. Moreover, rebels had destroyed many bridges, so aid organizations found it difficult to reach these financially and emotionally bankrupt refugees by road. They had to cut alternate paths through the bush, which took months.

To earn a little money, the Burundians accepted whatever jobs Congolese didn't care to do. To make matters worse, the Congolese government conscripted many of the stronger refugees to haul munitions to fight their rebels.

Large numbers of Burundians, especially children, died in the weeks following their arrival in Congo. Cholera took a huge toll on the refugees as did flies feasting on dead bodies from the war. Swarms attacked the refugees so ferociously that people walked with large palm branches as coverings against the voracious insects.

Before aid could reach the refugees, the threat of starvation loomed. In desperation, some young men returned to Burundi to beg food from those who remained. They crossed Lake Tanganyika at night and submerged their boats off shore by filling them with rocks, so the JRR would not spot them. They followed the river into the mountains where they hid in banana trees to avoid discovery, while relatives gathered food for family and friends in Congo. At night, the young men packed the food down to the shore, removed the rocks from their boats, and rowed back across the lake.

STARTING OVER

I've pieced together my family's early experiences in Congo from what Dad told me in later years and from what my older brother, Hari, remembers. Hari had not yet turned three years of age when he crossed Lake Tanganyika with Dad, Mum, and my one-year-old brother Josaphat. A female cousin named Bara crossed in the same boat and helped care for the two little boys.

Their boat landed at Ngovi, Congo. Burundian refugees flooded the shoreline. With rebels stealing food and attacking police stations in an attempt to destabilize the government, they did not feel safe. So Dad moved the family north to Mulongwe, with the intention of continuing north and entering Rwanda at its border with Congo. It seemed to him that Burundians who had fled to Rwanda found a better life. But something happened to halt their progress. Perhaps it was Josaphat reaching for some food in a boiling pot. The pot fell on the little boy, burning him severely and sending him to a makeshift clinic for treatment.

Whatever the reason, Dad reversed direction and took his family south, along Lake Tanganyika. They traveled back through Ngovi to a community known as Kabondozi, in the Fizi District. It was there, in 1974, that Mum delivered my first sister.

When Dad fled Burundi in 1972, he assumed the killings would stop within a couple of weeks. My family could then return to Gitaza and resume their comfortable life. This did not happen. Months later, my father received word that the situation in Burundi was worsening and many more were fleeing to the surrounding countries. Moreover, some of his employees had been assassinated when the killers could not locate him. His goods and property had been looted and occupied. This forced Dad to work at odd jobs in Congo to support his family.

Later in life, Dad told me how he made a wooden mortar for a Congolese man and received several bunches of bananas as his wages.

From that, he attempted to make a traditional Burundian drink. He put banana juice in a small wooden boat, covered it with banana leaves, and left it to ferment. One night, it rained heavily, and Dad assumed the drink was ruined. Two days later, he checked the boat which was full of juice. In Dad's opinion, rainwater mixing with the juice had weakened it, but a Congolese who sampled the juice raved about the great taste. He insisted it would sell.

From the sale of that juice, Dad purchased a new piece of African cloth for Mum who had just given birth to a baby girl. This is an important traditional gift for every woman who has just delivered a child. Not providing it would have meant great disgrace. Because of this unexpected provision at my sister's birth, she was called *Ntinyibagiye* meaning "God has not forgotten me." Her Christian name, by which I will refer to her from this point on, is Miriam.

ALWAYS AN ENTREPRENEUR

At Kabondozi, life changed for the better. My family received aid from Caritas, a Catholic relief agency, and Dad continued to look for odd jobs like hand-cultivating the Congolese' crops. As part of his pay, he got food for lunch and brought it home to share with the family. He used the money he earned with a hoe to buy and sell fish, which generated even more income.

Dad had moved to Kabondozi, in part, because he had heard that a famous Burundian pastor named Ciza had also fled to Congo and was living there. Dad visited Ciza on the same day as a Banyamulenge pastor named Kaganda came down from the mountains to call on Ciza.[1] My father developed a friendship with Pastor Kaganda who owned many cows. Later, he traveled to the mountains to see him. Dad did not have enough money to buy a cow, but with the little he had, and because Pastor Kaganda respected Pastor Ciza, he sold one of his cows to Dad on credit.

Arriving back on the shores of Lake Tanganyika, my father slaughtered the cow under a big tree and people came to buy meat for their households. Some butchers even came to buy larger pieces to go and sell elsewhere.

Dad then took the money back up the mountain to repay Pastor Kaganda. The pastor expressed surprise at how quickly he had been repaid and agreed to extend more credit. This was the beginning of a flourishing business between my father and the Banyamulenge cattle keepers that lasted many years.

From Kabondozi, my family moved further south to Mboko, in search of greater opportunity. Finally, around 1975, the United Nations ordered them to a refugee settlement known as Kenya-Tanganyika.[2] This land, on the shores of Lake Tanganyika, had been reserved by the Congolese government for Burundian refugees.

At that time, few Congolese lived in the vicinity. There was no source of drinking water, and the land had not been developed. The Burundian refugees had to build everything themselves. My brother Hari remembers the UN giving our family rations of ground nuts and flour while

---

1   Banyamulenge – a community of Rwandese from the Tutsi tribe having lived for many years in Congo and identifying more with their adopted country than their country of origin.
2   The Kenya-Tanganyika settlement was located near Nundu in the Fizi District of Congo. It is unrelated to the East African nation of Kenya.

we lived in Kenya-Tanganyika, and providing hoes to cultivate the land. With the first harvest, the food crisis ended. The government had granted each refugee family a plot of ground about half a hectare (about 1.2 acres) in size. Anything planted in the fertile soil grew well.

Some Burundians had managed to flee with their nets and returned to fishing for a living. The UN relief agency gave nets and starting capital to other refugees as well, to help them get started in the fishing business.

Dad resumed his meat business. As he walked through Kenya-Tanganyika selling his wares, my father would call out, "Throw away your vegetables and buy my meat and fish." For this reason, people nicknamed him *mwanga sombe* which means "throw out your cassava leaves"—the main vegetable consumed by Burundians and Congolese.

HARD LESSONS TO LEARN

In 1976, Mum birthed another baby girl named *Niyonganyirwa*. In Kirundi, this means "God is the one whom I cry out to." Her other name, by which I will refer to her from this point on, was Edisa.

As I mentioned earlier, my father had married two women. He fled Burundi with his second wife, Guenèse, my mum and the mother of my four siblings: Hari, Josaphat, Miriam, and Edisa.

Despite his former status in Burundi, Dad had learned to humble himself in Congo. Mum had not. After seven years as a refugee, she maintained the mindset of a queen in her palace. She always wanted to be served. She constantly asked for new clothes and special foods that her family's economic situation could not accommodate. This frustrated Dad. He did not know how to get his wife to accept the fact that things had changed.

At my birth in August 1979, he settled on a way to make sure Mum got the message. Drawing on the father's prerogative to name a child, Dad announced that I would be called *Shikajembe Twigimirimo Salama*. The first word means "get a hoe" in Swahili. The second word means "let's learn to work" in Kirundi. The third word is Swahili for "peace."

*　　*　　*

To this point in his life, my father had been a nominal Christian. Not long after my birth, he began to take his faith seriously. Influenced by the teaching of a spiritual woman revered for her prayers, Dad decided that polygamy had been a big mistake—one that he must rectify in order to please God.

Dad decided to return to his first wife, Nzobandora, in Burundi, while continuing to financially support his second wife, Guenèse, and us children in Congo. To detach from Mum physically, Dad built a separate house for her in our Kenya-Tanganyika compound.

Mum, who did not understand or accept the spiritual reason for his decision, lived in that house for a brief time before moving to the house of a man who already had a wife and children. She left me and my siblings in the hands of my father before I turned two years old. From then on, people began calling me *Innocent* because I was an innocent victim of war, of divorce, and of maltreatment toward refugees. Since I was an infant when this happened, I have no memory of Guenèse acting as a mother towards me. My earliest recollections of Mum date to a time when she was already living as wife and mother to her new family.

For years I resented Mum for leaving us. The only information I had about the causes of her departure was that she and Dad had fought. Even when I began to ask questions openly, no-one told me the truth about why she left. Traditional African culture does not allow adults to talk to children about family problems. So, I projected my anger on God because I was told by outsiders that Dad's conversion to Christianity caused my parents' separation. As an adult looking back, I imagine Mum must have felt betrayed and abandoned.

Watching my friends' mothers caring and cooking for them greatly troubled me. At home, Dad and my two elder brothers shared all these tasks. I felt underprivileged and deprived of the benefits that other children enjoyed. I had a distant mother who lived in the same village and was being Mum to other children she birthed after remarriage. Whenever I argued with my friends and they wanted to hurt me, they would say things like, "That's why your mother abandoned you." They could have said nothing more devastating.

ABANDONED

After my Mum left, Dad's first wife Nzobandora came to Congo to live with us. When Dad fled Burundi, she had moved away to marry another man, but she had returned and was staying on my father's property in Gitaza when she learned of his desire to reunite. Though skeptical at first, she traveled to Congo within a week of Guenèse leaving the family compound. As my sister Miriam recalls, Nzobandora stayed with our family for several months before returning to Burundi. She was ill for much of that time.

Between my second and third birthdays, Dad decided to return to Burundi to join Nzobandora, to repossess his properties, and to make arrangements for the repatriation of his whole family. For almost a decade, his houses, businesses, and farms had been occupied by old friends and neighbors. Dad thought the repossession process would take just a few days, since everyone knew him. But the occupants had no intention of giving up these properties despite their acknowledgement that Dad owned them.

Over a period of two years, Dad's former friends used bureaucratic tricks to delay the repossession process. All the while they planned to eliminate him. Toward the end of this time, Nzobandora died. The two children my father had with her, together with their maternal uncles, blamed Dad for her death. As a Christian, Dad had refused to take his wife to witchdoctors who, they said, might have healed her.

Finally, when no one was willing to defend him and even the government helped his opponents confiscate his property, my traumatized father became mentally unstable.

*   *   *

Meanwhile, I lived with my two brothers and two sisters on our compound in Congo. Dad had left us in the care and supervision of neighbors, but they proved to be more interested in the palm and banana trees on his property than in meeting his children's basic needs. So Hari, who was not yet fourteen years of age, looked after us. "I caught lots of fish," recalls my brother. "Half of my catch I exchanged for cassava flour and the rest we ate at home." We used the cassava flour to make *ugali*, a staple food throughout much of Africa. The banana trees Dad had planted also provided a source of food, and although she had responsibilities elsewhere, our mother helped us by maintaining our cassava garden.

The rest of us tried to help where we could. One day, I followed my older sister Miriam to the shores of Lake Tanganyika to fish, and a large crocodile came out of the water. Curious, I wanted to get a little closer to the beast, but Miriam pulled me away, and we ran home as fast as we could. Miriam remembers the experience to this day, probably because she got in trouble for what drew her to the lakeshore in the first place. In that culture, it was taboo for a woman to fish.

After a year or two of Hari's parenting, we began making regular visits to the home of my cousin Magdalene and her husband, Samuel Bazira, which was located about 200 meters from ours. Whenever we walked into the Baziras' house, Magdalene would ask, "Have you eaten?" When we said we had not, she would go to the back of the house and begin preparing food for us—whether or not they had already finished their meal. This went on for a long time. Then one day the Baziras said, "Please come to our house early so we don't have to cook twice, and you can eat with us." They had an empty room in their home and sometimes, after feeding us, they suggested we stay overnight.

> *Read "Sharing Food with Ducks" on page 155 for a word-picture of mealtime in a refugee settlement.*

Finally, they just took the five of us into their home. For a period of two years, the Baziras cared for us and comforted our broken hearts, since my father had not returned from Burundi. Their oversight largely released Hari from his parenting responsibilities, although he continued to fish.

Rev. Bazira pastored a Free Methodist church in the Kenya-Tanganyika refugee settlement. He and Magdalene raised us alongside their three surviving biological children. Five of Rev. Bazira's siblings also lived with them, so the entire household consisted of fourteen people.

The Baziras taught us Christian principles and good behavior, both in society and at home. Rev. Bazira's income did not sufficiently cover the needs of this expanded household, but we witnessed God's provision in many ways. Magdalene kept cassava gardens and made *ubuswage*, a traditional Burundian cassava bread. She also planted rice and grew a little maize. Hari, Josaphat, and Miriam helped with the manual labor, including selling the cassava bread. Besides being a pastor, Rev. Bazira also fished for a living, as did Hari and Josaphat. Hari, in particular, persistently and selflessly worked to bring home whatever he could at the end of each day so we would always have something to eat.

While living with the Baziras, I enrolled in a Free Methodist primary school that catered to both refugee and Congolese children. At first, I was so excited to be at school. I had always been curious. "You were very clever and asked so many questions," said my sister Miriam years later. "Everything you saw you wanted to understand." I had dreams of becoming a leader who would redeem Burundi and Africa from its injustice. For this reason, I had no problem waking up at dawn to bathe in the waters of Lake Tanganyika and brush my teeth with the white sand of the beach before setting off for school.

One week later, however, I felt restricted by the school's rules. These rules included whippings for students who talked in class, failed to answer a test question correctly, or arrived late. Sometimes I lied about being sick and went fishing in the lake instead. But when I did, my brothers and relatives whipped me as a way of encouraging me to keep my education on track. We had to walk one hour from our village to the school, and I tried my best not to be late, to avoid the inevitable punishment.

Though the Free Methodist Church operated our school, each student's family had to pay tuition, and we refugees didn't always have the money. I recall one compassionate teacher who risked his job by letting those of us who couldn't pay climb into his classroom through a window so we could continue to learn. He loved teaching religion, and students in his class prayed and sang with passion. I still remember drumming on the desk while we sang—similar to clapping in worship today.

I believe my brother Hari wanted me to get as much education as possible because he had not been able to finish. While parenting his siblings, he had difficulty concentrating on schoolwork and had to repeat a lot of classes. Hari eventually dropped out of secondary school.

> *Refugees experience both rejection and acceptance in their host countries. For a taste of both, read "Animosity toward Newcomers" on page 157.*

DAD RETURNS

As I progressed in school, concerned relatives in Burundi pooled their money and took my father to a mental hospital in Bujumbura. There he began to get well. When the hospital released him, Dad spent two months with relatives in Gitaza to ensure his full recovery. Then, he returned to his children in Congo. I had entered my second year of primary school when Dad came back.

Dad arrived in Congo a very weak and unstable man. His hands and feet carried scars from having been chained while in hospital. Sometimes at night he would wake up and scream. The more he recovered, though, the more my father began to interact with us. He joined in the collection of fish and took them to the Banyamulenge community in the mountains to sell. As Dad regained his health, life improved because he was very good at business and people trusted him.

When Dad returned to Congo, my two brothers and my oldest sister Miriam had already moved back to our family's compound. They wanted to protect the land, which was fertile and had palm trees, against those plotting to confiscate it.[3] Someone had been living in our old house, and the grass roof had caught fire, so we had to rebuild it. My siblings paddled a canoe down the lakeshore to cut trees and bring them back to construct the beams for our new mud and wood house.

My sister Edisa and I stayed at the Baziras' place until the return of our father. The thought of having Dad back excited me. Although I cried bitterly when other children made fun of me, saying that I had a mad father, I felt encouraged by his presence. In fact, Dad soon recovered completely. Even the wounds on his hands and feet, from the chains used to restrain his fury towards those occupying his properties in Burundi, had healed.

Soon after arriving back in Congo, Dad called on my mother Guenèse and explained to her that because Nzobandora had died, he would now be able to take her as his legitimate wife. Mum rejected his proposal, however, and Dad remained single for more than fifteen years.

---

3   Palm trees yielded large bunches of plum-sized fruit from which we cooked, pressed, and re-fined reddish palm oil used for cooking. Separately, we milled palm kernels to extract oil used in soaps and cosmetics.

I was very close to my father and spent time with him whenever possible. I followed Dad as he resumed his multiple trades—buying and selling fish, cows, and bananas.

At some point, however, I developed the habit of stealing money from Dad. I started by taking a small amount, just enough to buy sweets. But my habitual thievery grew over time. I felt guilty about stealing from Dad, but I could not come out in the open with it. Things got so bad that Dad could not trust me anymore. He never showed hatred towards me, only towards my bad behavior.

Dad tried many ways to help me stop stealing, but his methods did not succeed until the day he began to trust in me again. Dad even sent me into the mountains with money for two cows he had purchased on credit. I had to walk about eight hours and spend at least one night there. Little by little, I lost my love of money, and my relationship with my father was restored.

My sister Edisa, three years older than me, was very skillful. She would always find ways of making money—even as a school girl. For example, she bought cheap fruit from villagers and she made donuts, selling both to her schoolmates during recess. Early in primary school, before I changed my ways, I remember stealing money to buy fruit and walk around with it during recess. This was a status symbol at a time and in a culture when no concept of school lunches existed. Eventually, Edisa passed her business skills to me. By my ninth birthday, I bought some second-hand clothes with money I had honestly earned.

In 1991, at the age of 13, Edisa had just graduated sixth grade with plans to attend secondary school. Suddenly, she developed an intense headache and a high fever. We bought medicine, but within two days she could no longer talk. Some in our village thought she had been bewitched. My family, with the help of our neighbors, transported Edisa more than 7 kilometers (about 4½ miles) on an improvised stretcher to the hospital at Nundu.[4] I found out about this because I met the people carrying the stretcher as I was on my way home from school.

Edisa died the next day. Her loss left our family speechless and very sad.

LEAVING OUR REFUGE WITH HOPE OF PEACE

In 1992, the Burundian government agreed to a multi-party democracy. This brought great hope to the oppressed Hutu majority. FRODEBU (Front pour la democratie au Burundi) was a leading opposition party, supported mainly by Hutus, but by some Tutsis as well. Melchior Ndadaye led the party. Ndadaye had fled Burundi in 1972 as a twelve-year-old and had recently returned to Burundi from a refugee camp in Rwanda. Though Hutus supported him wholeheartedly, we never dreamed that Ndadaye's *redemption* agenda would succeed in our country when Tutsis occupied over 95 percent of the national army and key governmental positions.

During the election campaign in Burundi, the refugees in Congo held fervent prayer meetings, asking God to grant favor to the Hutu-supported party. We followed the election news on radio, and the number of citizens voting in the June 1993 election proved the hunger for change in Burundi.

---

4   The refugee ambulance: Men cut two small trees to form the poles and stretched a canvas between them. Everyone would stop what they were doing to help carry the improvised stretcher and transport a sick person.

As the radio announcer declared the FRODEBU party had won, cheers of victory rose in every corner of Congo where Burundian refugees lived. That night our fishermen did not venture out onto the lake as usual. Instead, they carried their oil lamps through the villages while singing victory songs about going home and the end of suffering. This went on until dawn.

Our excitement and exhilaration lasted for days and evolved to near-madness while people drank to excess and uprooted crops from their gardens as a statement that they were now going home and would no longer have anything to do with Congo. It blew the refugees' minds to think that we would be able to return home without a war, but simply by a free and fair election, to a country where justice had been absent for decades. We could hardly believe the ruling party had accepted the election results marking their defeat. It seemed as if sky and earth had traded places. Those things we could only fantasize about before had now become reality.

The excitement among refugees could not be denied, yet some elderly refugees doubted that the current government would actually give up power. Their doubts appeared unfounded on July 10, 1993, at the inauguration of Melchior Ndadaye as president of Burundi.

On that day, the Burundian refugees in our area of eastern Congo slaughtered a huge cow to celebrate the victory. Many refugees immediately began selling their properties in Congo at very low prices, trying to get whatever they could before making the journey home. Some even destroyed crops they couldn't sell so the Congolese would not benefit. Few had the patience to wait until the Office of the United Nations High Commissioner for Refugees (UNHCR) made official arrangements to repatriate them.

Instead, we crossed the lake without permission, just as my family had done when they came to Congo.

On August 1, 1993, soon after my brother Josaphat's wedding, I climbed with my cousins into a boat bound for Burundi, for the first time in my life. The time was exactly 10:00 p.m.

For more on a refugee's desire to return home, read "UNHCR: Caring for Refugees" on page 161.

CHAPTER 3

Dashed Hopes

Anticipation filled my heart as the bow of our small motorboat split the quiet waters of Lake Tanganyika. A full moon rose and a cool wind blew softly in my face as I thought of all the good things my home country had to offer. Three hours after leaving Congo, we arrived at the Burundian shoreline, near Magara. The authorities would not allow us to disembark at night, so we remained on the boat until morning. I wore warm clothes against the chilly night air but was unable to sleep. I was too excited.

With the dawn, I could see cars driving by on the coastal road. I began counting them, as a means of comparing Burundi to Congo. In just a few moments, my count equaled the number that passed on the coastal road of Congo in an entire month.

Around 6:00 a.m., we boarded a minibus going north to Gitaza, the village of my father's birth. He still owned two houses and a sizeable plot of land in that community. On our arrival, I met many relatives who had heard about me but never seen me. They showed me love, and it seemed to me that I had finally arrived where I should have been all my life.

As I surveyed the beautiful country I would now call my own, I could hardly believe we had been forced to live in a country like Congo where the locals despised us. In Congo, we had to travel four kilometers to fetch drinking water from a river, but in Gitaza drinking water flowed from common taps. The main road through Nundu had been dirty and full of pot holes, but a paved road ran through Gitaza. We Burundians had so many things of which to be proud.

One week later, Dad, my brother Hari, and my sister Miriam joined me in Burundi. For the time being, my brother Josaphat decided to remain in Congo with his new wife, Cizanye. Our family moved into one of Dad's houses. The person who had occupied it illegally had left soon after President Ndadaye officially assumed power.

MY NAME CHANGE

I had arrived in Burundi after passing primary school exams in Congo, but since my Kirundi did not meet the level of proficiency of the local kids, I had to go back to primary school in order to continue with my studies in Burundi. Moreover, the Burundian government did not value Congo's education system which they viewed as full of corruption.

In September, I enrolled at the Rutunga primary school as a fourth year student. Though embarrassed at having to repeat three grades I knew this would give me an opportunity to learn more about my country.

On the first day of school, my teacher wanted to find out if I was a Burundian or a Congolese, because my name, Shikajembe Innocent (a Swahili name and a French name) offered no hints as to my Burundian roots.[1] The teacher advised me to change the Swahili name to a Kirundi name in order to be identified as a Burundian. The idea sounded perfect to me. Many times over the years we lived in Congo I had asked my father to change my name as it referred to my mother and not me. The children in Congo used to tease me for being called "get a hoe." That name conveyed an outdated message since Mum had learned to farm, and she was also no longer my father's wife.

As I returned home from school, I visited my aunt (the elder sister of my father) who would understand both what the teacher meant and my desire to have my name changed. She did understand. She also suggested the name Magambi, the name of her grandfather. Magambi comes from the Kirundi word *migambi* meaning "projects, plans or advice."

"No one in the family has ever taken that name," she assured me.

The name sounded wonderful to me. I repeated it many times over as I went to find my father and explain the whole matter. Dad would have preferred my Swahili name translated into Kirundi, but since his elder sister had already suggested the other name, he simply said, *Ni bibe nkuko yavuze* meaning "Let what she said be so."

I jumped for joy and walked around our village repeating my new name until it spread like wildfire.[2]

---

1   My two other names, Twigimirimo and Salama, did not appear on my school registration documents.
2   In the West, changing a name would require a legal procedure, but I had no form of ID until age 27, so changing names was simply a matter of letting those around me know what I would be called from that day forward.

MORE TROUBLE

Every day, more refugees returned to Burundi from numerous camps in nations bordering the tiny East African country. Like me, some had been born in exile. The parents of many of these second-generation refugees had died, so they had great difficulty identifying their family homes.

Some refugees came with revenge in their hearts, brandishing machetes to chase out of their houses those who had occupied them— instead of going through the protocol set up by the new government. In some cases, people killed other people while trying to resolve owner-ship disputes.

Still, the inauguration of Melchoir Ndadaye gave hope to many Burundians that the country's economy would rise and the living condi-tions of the general populace would improve as elected officials exercised good governance. Unfortunately, President Ndadaye wasn't given much time to carry out his platform of respect between all ethnic groups.

*   *   *

Having won Burundi's first free and fair multi-party election by a landslide, President Ndadaye appointed several opposition candidates to his government. But he also implemented measures which threatened the economic interests of the Tutsi elite and Tutsi control of the military. At the same time, thousands of Hutu families who had fled Burundi after the 1972 killings had begun to return. They expected their houses and lands back. In a largely agricultural economy, this left many Tutsi families home-less and without provision for life.

Only three months into his presidency, the military staged a coup in

Burundi's capital city, Bujumbura. During the take-over, they assassinated President Ndadaye along with nine ministers and members of parliament.

*   *   *

The word *devastated* aptly describes the spiritual and emotional condition of the refugee community as news of the assassination spread. For years we had hoped to breathe the air of freedom in our country, yet hatred still ravaged Burundian hearts. The act of accepting the election results had been purely superficial. Deep inside, many Burundians held a very different attitude. For them the old sayings rang true: "The Tutsi will let the Hutu hold the machete; but the Hutu should hold the sharp, metal end, while the Tutsi holds onto the wooden handle for both of them." Another similar saying translates like this, "The Tutsi will let the Hutu rule as long as the barrel of the gun is sealed."[3]

Following the assassination, the threat of death once again invaded everyday life. In view of this unbearable situation, some Hutus decided to flee to neighboring countries while others chose to stay. Although we had only been in Burundi for four months, Dad did not want to wait. He urged us to join Josaphat back in Congo.

Returning to Congo proved to be painful beyond what we could have expected or imagined. We honestly wondered if God had turned His back on us. How else could He allow us to face so much pain and injustice?

Those refugees who left Congo after selling their properties and

---

3   This saying refers to the imperative of maintaining a majority Tutsi army, even with a majority Hutu government.

destroying their crops suffered the most. They survived only on what UNHCR provided. Dad had not sold his main property in Congo, which had palm trees on it.[4] This gave us a source of income when we had to flee to Congo a second time. We could also host others who ran away from Burundi and joined us.

Arriving back in Congo, I learned that I had passed my sixth grade exams, which made me eligible to start secondary school. But we returned in December, so I had to wait to begin my studies until September when the next academic year would start.

LIFE LESSONS LEARNED

During the wait, I traveled with Dad as he resumed his business of trading fish and buying goats and cows from the Banyamulenge people in the mountainous areas of Kakuma, Bibogobogo, and Rutabura. Looking back on these days, I cherish the opportunities our journeys gave me to learn things from him that have greatly benefited me in adulthood.

For instance, he told me how and where he began to get serious about his Christian faith and realized that having more than one wife or more than one sexual partner was wrong. Although his change in thinking eventually resulted in estrangement from my mother, I now can appreciate Dad's desire to live a God-honoring life.

Then one day Dad said, "Innocent, I want you to get a haircut, dress properly, and be ready for me to take you somewhere in four days." At age fourteen, it struck me as strange that my father would give me this

---

4   Skeptical that changes in Burundi would last, my brother Josaphat had advised against rushing to sell this property, though potential buyers had already been identified.

much advance notice of a journey with him. If we went to the mountains, sometimes Dad would tell me the day before, but more likely he would wake me at 3:00 a.m. and say, "Let's go." So Dad telling me to be ready this far in advance made me very anxious.

The day came, and we began walking at about 2:00 p.m. We walked from our village, Kenya-Tanganyika, to a nearby village called Kenya-Kangeta. As we walked, Dad lectured me on the subject of sexual purity and the importance of abstaining until marriage. Then he explained to me how, in the past, parents chose wives for their sons. "They looked not only at the girl's physical appearance," he said, "but at the character of her parents and her siblings." The parents also inquired of the neighbors about the girl. Sometimes, Dad said, if the girl looked too clean, it was a sign of laziness; but if a girl had a little dirt on her, it meant she was a hard worker. Occasionally, the parents would ask the girl for water, noting the time it took to fetch the water and whether the cup was clean.

If the girl seemed suitable, the parents would pay the bridal price and inform their son, "We have found your wife." Though some parents misused their prerogative to grant favors to friends, and so forth, much of the time it worked well.

Dad said he had been thinking of me and my marriage, and had been closely watching a girl in Kenya-Kangeta. He then admitted that he was taking me to meet that girl and her family. My heart skipped a beat. I never imagined Dad would introduce me to someone he expected me to marry—not at fourteen years of age. What about my dreams of becoming an influential leader?

Knowing I could speak openly with him, I asked, "What about my education?" Dad assured me he didn't intend for me to get married right away. He simply wanted to introduce me to the girl—for the future. Dad then revealed to me his concern that I would end up like he had, with more than one wife.

Stating that he wasn't encouraging me to be sexually active, Dad added, "But if you do, it is better to fix your eyes on one girl and eventually marry her."

As it turned out, the girl and her mother knew I was coming and had fixed a meal for us. The mother of the thirteen-year-old girl had been widowed for as long as the girl had been alive, without having become promiscuous, unlike most other widows. For this very reason, Dad thought highly of her character. After we ate and started back, I told my father I would give him an answer. I never did. Although he explained his intentions to me, I was very disappointed at what Dad had done. Yet, the lesson of purity stuck in my mind.

BACK TO BURUNDI

At age fourteen, Dad sent me back to Burundi to help resolve a family matter. An older cousin had married a young Congolese woman named Mwenge. My cousin's father lived in Burundi, so everyone considered Dad to be my cousin's guardian in Congo.

Mwenge's family threatened Dad, claiming the couple had moved in together without the bridal price being paid. But whenever Dad paid the bridal price to one set of the girl's relatives, another set would arrive at our door claiming they had not received their share. Then, Dad had to pay something to appease them.

After this scenario repeated several times, other so-called relatives came from the city of Uvira in Congo claiming to be the real uncle and father of the girl. They didn't want to hear anything about what had been given earlier. They demanded the full bridal price for their daughter. At the same time, these people wanted to take her home because they deemed it ridiculous for a Burundian to marry their daughter.[5] Moreover, Mwenge was about fourteen years old and my cousin, over thirty, had already had many wives.

Dad did not know how to handle the situation. My cousin had already escaped to Burundi with Mwenge. Someone had to go to Burundi and report the issue to our extended family. Since none of my brothers wanted to go, I volunteered for the task. I certainly did not want to see my father go to Burundi and risk being traumatized again.

In early April 1994, I boarded a boat crossing Lake Tanganyika, and for the second time in less than one year, I stepped out of the watercraft onto Burundian soil.

Learn about the Tutsi persecution that followed President Ndadaye's death. Read "Hope Remains despite the Pain" on page 165.

* * *

Reacting to the killing of President Ndadaye in October 1993, local Hutu officials, aided by extremists in the general population, had rounded up and executed many Tutsi citizens in

---

5   Prejudice against refugees thrived, not because the Congolese had more wealth or education but simply because they lived on their forefathers' land while we Burundians came begging asylum.

rural areas. The army, aided by Tutsi extremists, responded to these kill-ings by conducting reprisal attacks on Hutus. The Red Cross estimates that 100,000 citizens, both Hutu and Tutsi, died in those early days after the assassination. In January 1994, the National Assembly had elected FRODEBU's Cyprien Ntaryamira, the former minister of agriculture, as president of Burundi. Just before I returned to Burundi, however, Ntaryamira died in a plane crash, along with Rwandan president Juvenal Habyarimana. That event, occurring on April 8, 1994, sparked the infa-mous Rwandan genocide.

Instability reigned across the African Great Lakes Region. In returning to Burundi, I witnessed the beginning of a civil war that lasted until 2005 and cost an estimated 300,000 lives.

*   *   *

A dangerous situation confronted me in Burundi. When I left Congo, I knew my country was embroiled in violence, but I had heard that it was sporadic—not a daily occurrence. Immediately upon arriving in Gitaza, however, I heard rumors of Hutus in the surrounding hills undergo-ing informal military training and of their plan to form a rebel army. Rumors also spread of a planned attack on the rebels by the Burundian army. Fear gripped me as I hurried to accomplish my task.

A few days before my planned return to Congo, I slept in my Cousin Vincent's compound at Gitaza. An advisor to the local administrator, Vincent had gone into hiding for fear the army was coming to arrest or kill community leaders. At 3:00 a.m., I woke at the sound of gunfire. Thinking our compound was under attack, I made up my mind to flee to the mountain village in which my mother had been born.

Dressed only in a pair of shorts and with my T-shirt and sandals in hand, I climbed the hill in the back of the compound. I did not know where the shots had come from, only that I had to get away. A clear night sky and a cool breeze greeted me as I ran past ghostly fields of cassava, and later, up treeless mountain paths strewn with rocks.

Unbeknownst to me, I ran directly at the gunfire rather than away from it. *Hagarara!* "Stop!" barked a voice in the darkness. The voice ordered me to the ground, and I had no difficulty obeying. My knees gave way, and I fell on my face. The voice ordered me to let go of whatever I had in my right hand, and I obeyed, releasing my shoes and shirt.

Then I heard another commanding voice from the same direction. *Muzane ino!* "Bring him over here." Willing all my strength, I rose fearfully and walked toward the second voice as the first voice circled round, following me from behind. I fully expected to be shot in the back at any moment.

Reaching the top of the hill, I came face to face with Tutsi Army Captain Gilbert Niyonkuru and more than thirty soldiers. They had surrounded a house owned by Mr. Nimbona Athanase, a Hutu accused of teaching military skills to young men. The captain had stationed half of his soldiers at the front gate, facing Lake Tanganyika. The other half of his forces secured the back of the house, facing the mountain. My escort ordered me to sit next to the captain, who occupied a space on the *khonde,* the outside patio at the corner of the house. Flanked by two armed guards, the captain himself held a pistol at the ready.

Captain Niynkuru interrogated me:

"What made you run?"

"Where were you running to?"

"Where is your father and what does he do?"

"Do you know anyone involved in military training?"

"Have you participated in Athanase's military coaching?"

At this point, I considered myself a dead man. I honestly do not remember answering any of the questions intelligibly. Severely shaken by the shooting going on around me, my teeth chattered, and I experienced a nearly uncontrollable urge to empty my bowels. Wondering why my obedience to my father had attracted this extreme punishment rather than a reward, I called on the name of Jesus not to save me any longer, but to allow me to enter heaven. I had lost all hope.

What I did not know at the time (and it was good that I didn't) was that these same soldiers had killed a teenage boy just before capturing me. They suspected the young man of being Mr. Athanase's body guard, and it was by the mercy of God that I wasn't shot while running.

I also did not know, as I sat quivering on the cold concrete patio, that the soldiers were continuing to fire their guns in the air in hopes of provoking a response from the rebel group; they did not get one. Finally, around 5:00 a.m., the captain called someone to catalog the weapons retrieved from the dead young man: a Kalashnikov rifle, a rifle-launched grenade, and a few bullets. Shortly after that, my captors released me.

Descending the hill, I observed thousands of people carrying babies and luggage. They moved slowly up the mountain, carefully watching the government soldiers. After President Ndadaye's assassination by the military the previous October, cabinet ministers and members of parliament had been granted refuge in the capital city's foreign embassies. The general population had no such refuge, so they began to refer to the high places as "embassies" and many Hutus fled there in the months that followed.

Back in Gitaza, I determined not to spend another night here; I took a bus to Magara where I could board a boat for Congo. Sadly, I did not have enough money to buy passage, and I was forced to return to Gitaza the very next day to borrow from family members. Around 2:00 p.m., as I prepared to board yet another bus to Magara, I witnessed my captors of the previous day bringing the wife of Athanase into town. The soldiers left her in the hands of Jacques Karabagega, the district commissioner of Muhuta, with instructions to keep her in prison until they found her husband.

Soon after, Hutu rebels trained by Athanase came to ask Mr. Karabagega to release the woman. Mr. Karabagega, himself a Hutu, knew that his faithfulness to his people and his disobedience to the soldiers could cost him his life. Nevertheless, he released the woman, wrote a letter of resignation, and escaped to Congo that same night.

One week later, Tutsi soldiers looted and burned to the ground all the houses where the district commissioner and other Hutu officials had lived.

For the second time in one year, I fled my country.

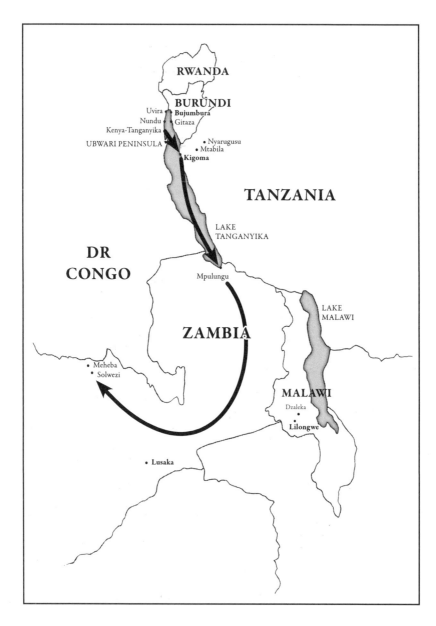

Innocent's Journey at Age 17

CHAPTER 4

Teenager on the Run

Arriving back in Congo, I found my twenty-three-year-old brother Josaphat preparing to leave for Burundi to bring me back. He had heard of the deteriorating security and was worried about me. My family expressed first shock and then great joy as I told them about my brush with death and how God had protected me. Although it meant leaving my beloved Burundi once more, returning to the arms of my loved ones felt wonderful.

I started secondary school in Congo at age fifteen in September of 1994. About the same time, members of our extended family fleeing the ongoing violence in Burundi began to arrive at our compound on the western shores of Lake Tanganyika. At one point, we sheltered fifty-three people in our five small mud-brick buildings. Providing for these new refugees wasn't easy. We had limited income, but time after time we saw God supply what we needed. Sometimes we would receive food through the World Food Program. Sometimes we received no outside aid, but through a combination of odd jobs and fishing we survived in the relative safety of our refugee settlement.

That safety would soon evaporate. Two years later, fighting erupted in our host country. In September 1996, a cohort of rebel groups started a war against the government of President Joseph Mobutu. Many Congolese living in the trading center of Uvira to the north passed through our settlement as they ran away from the conflict.

As the fighting moved closer to Kenya-Tanganyika, some refugees decided to leave and others opted to stay and try to protect their property. Several of the young people in our community joined the Mai-Mai,[1] which fought the rebels alongside (and often in place of) Mobutu's unpaid and disillusioned army.

Besides acting as a local, loosely organized military force, the Mai-Mai promoted indigenous animistic practices such as washing with certain herbs to render the body bullet-proof, as well as rubbing those herbs into the body through cuts on the skin or wearing charms. The Mai-Mai believed these charms could also make a wearer disappear when encircled by enemies, just by touching a tree.

The Mai-Mai invited everyone in our village to join in these protective practices. As a Christian, Dad refused to allow his family to engage in the animistic rites, as it meant putting one's hope and trust in charms rather than in God. My brother Josaphat, a preacher, would not involve

---

1   Mai-Mai is the name given to community-based militia groups fighting in what is today the Democratic Republic of Congo.

himself with the Mai-Mai, but my older brother Hari joined as a means of protection.

Dad knew I was struggling to decide. He advised me many times against joining the Mai-Mai, thinking fear could easily push me towards them. Because of my near-death experience in Burundi, however, all I wanted to do was get away from the fighting, and from that point on I searched for any possible way to leave Congo.

PLANNING MY ESCAPE

In those days, Dad sold meat to the endless columns of people fleeing the fighting, as they passed through our village. Some were Burundian or Rwandese fleeing from other refugee camps. Some were citizens of Congo trying to escape the war. I worked closely with my father, holding the cash bag he used to conduct business—although Congolese currency suffered from such high inflation that many of the notes in the bag carried little value.

But my attention was not on what my father was doing or on my part in helping advance his business. Dad could see my distraction, and one day he asked me, "Why are you so distant?"

"I want to leave Congo," I confessed. "Please give me money so I can go."

"You cannot go alone, Innocent," Dad replied. "You are only seventeen. You must wait until one of your older brothers decides to flee and take you with him."[2] Hoping to pacify me, he gave me US$5 and some Congolese pocket money.

---

2   For his part, my father was set on never being a refugee in another country. He chose to either die in Congo or return to Burundi and await his death in his homeland.

I soon found my means of escape, however. One of my cousins owned a fishing boat, and the leader of a large Hutu political group, the Palipehutu, approached him and asked to be rowed to the Ubwari Peninsula.[3] I knew how to row, so I jumped at the chance to leave Kenya-Tanganyika under the pretense of helping smuggle this high-profile politician. Dad agreed, assuming I would help my cousin and then return because he (my father) had not given me permission to leave and because I did not have enough money to go anywhere. Still, the voyage involved some danger. The Banyamulenge rebels controlled the area in which we lived and would have shot any Hutu refugee from either Rwanda or Burundi.

Once we reached the peninsula with our human cargo, I informed my cousin that I would not go back with him. After a prolonged and heated discussion, he finally left.

DESTINATION TANZANIA

I stayed for two days on the peninsula waiting for the opportunity to board a motorboat going to Tanzania. I knew I would not be able to afford paying a normal fare which would have cost between US$50 and US$100 because of the high demand for this means of escape and the scarcity of fuel.

Amazingly I soon met another cousin who had been hired by his boss to transport family members to the peninsula by fishing boat, and beyond that to Tanzania. I pleaded with my relative to take me across

---

3   Petrol supplies dried up with the beginning of the war, so the only means of escaping the mainland was by an oar-powered fishing boat to the Ubwari Peninsula where a motorboat could be hired.

the lake to Tanzania, but he protested. "Even those who have paid full fare won't be able to fit in my boat," he told me.[4] Still, my cousin told me what time in the night they would board and offered me this hope. "You could try to take advantage of the darkness to get into the boat and hide," he said.

At the appointed time, I waited in the dark until some of the boss's family started to board and then pretended to be part of the group. A couple hours into the crossing, they discovered me and the boss started shouting at me and demanding money. I gave him what I had—around US$5. This small amount infuriated him, and he declared his intention to throw me overboard.

Falling to my knees, I begged the man, "Please do not kill me."

"If you keep me on board," I pleaded, "I will ask Reverend Samuel Bazira to pay for my fare on our arrival in Tanzania." My cousin, who was steering the boat, testified that I was telling the truth. We landed in Kigoma, Tanzania on November 10, 1996.

Rev. Bazira's family, who had arrived in Tanzania the previous year, was so happy to see me. They immediately paid my fare across the lake.

OFF TO MALAWI

Although displaced from their native Burundi and now from their refuge in Congo, the Bazira family lived in Kigoma, a major port and city in western Tanzania, rather than a refugee camp. So many people

---

4   People wanting to cross from the Ubwari Peninsula to Tanzania far exceeded available boats. When transporting family, owners hid their boats and traveled at night to avoid being commandeered by someone in authority.

were fleeing from Congo to Tanzania that the government did not want them to live in the towns and cities. They ordered all refugees to settle in refugee camps according to their nationalities. To enforce this order, the police arrested any refugees found in the country's western municipalities and transported them to the camps.

But refugees like the Baziras who had found employment or started businesses in these municipalities did not want to relocate to the camps. Moreover, the Tanzanian government had allocated bush areas for refugees to work on until they became habitable, and news from the camps told of water shortages, cholera, and snakes. For the brief time I lived with the Baziras, we lived in the constant fear of being arrested and relocated to these camps.

At the same time, we heard encouraging news from Malawi's Dzaleka Refugee Camp, located 1,600 kilometers (994 miles) by bus southeast of Kigoma. Refugees arriving at that camp reported receiving a monthly allowance toward rent and food, and students received help to continue their education.

The Baziras insisted I go to Malawi to find better opportunities. They began to inquire how much it would cost to send me part of the way by ship, along the eastern shores of Lake Tanganyika. Someone told them a ticket would cost 4,000 Tanzanian shillings, so they gave me 10,000. As it turned out, that wasn't nearly enough. A ticket on the ship cost 9,000 shillings. I also had to buy a Tanzanian temporary travel permit and a bus ticket to my final destination once I left the ship.

Nevertheless, on December 25, 1996, I boarded the *MV Mwongozo* for the first leg of the journey to Malawi.

DETOUR TO ZAMBIA

I knew no one on the ship, nor did I know the names of any towns or cities we would pass as we traveled south along the Tanzanian coastline—only the port where I would disembark. I also did not know that I should have purchased my ticket in advance. After boarding the *Mwongozo*, I expected to pay my fare once the ship got underway. To my dismay, immigration officers began checking each passenger's ticket and travel permit—which I did not have. What could I do?

While waiting to be discovered, I heard someone in the crowd speaking a Congolese dialect called Kibembe. I had been born and lived all of my life among the Bembe people, so I greeted them in this language. They, in turn, introduced me to their friends—a mixed group of Burundian and Congolese refugees. When they learned I was alone, they invited me to travel with them. Together, we made some contributions toward the fare, the temporary travel permits, and a bribe that kept us on the ship despite the immigration officers' mandate to arrest illegal travelers.

During the two-day-long voyage along the eastern shore of Lake Tanganyika, this Burundian/Congolese community fed me and included me in their plans to disembark at a Tanzanian town called Kirando 2. There, we could board a bus for the final leg of our journey to Malawi.

As we prepared to get off the *Mwongozo*, however, other refugees standing on shore shouted at us in Kifulero, another Congolese dialect. *Mutashonoke, mutashonoke akugwatana!* "Don't get off, don't get off—they are arresting people!" Hearing this, we moved back inside the ship. We collected more money and sent our community representative to pay more fares and bribes, which enabled us to continue on to Zambia.

The last port along the Tanzanian coastline at which we could disembark without international passports was Kasanga. There we boarded a large open boat to Mpulungu, Zambia. This boat made daytime, scheduled trips to and from Mpulungu, transporting people wanting to buy or sell goods across the Tanzanian/Zambian border. The authorities expected all non-Zambians without a passport to leave Mpulungu by the time the last boat departed each evening.

In Mpulungu, our Burundian/Congolese community split in two. Those with money to continue their journey to Malawi booked themselves at a simple guest house for the night and planned to resume their travels in the morning. Others like me, without money, had no choice but to report to the Zambian police and ask for asylum on the pretense that we had arrived straight from war-torn Congo. We feared being forced back to Tanzania had we told them the truth—that we did not want to live in that county's refugee camps and that some of us were, in fact, Burundian.

The Zambian police took us to a transit station where they held asylum seekers waiting to be transferred to refugee camps. The guards at this transit station gave each of us a meal and a blanket to sleep on the floor, but they gave us something even more valuable—hope. They began telling us about the comfortable living conditions we would find at Meheba Refugee Settlement.

We were in a border community in northeastern Zambia—about 1,250 kilometers (777 miles) distant from the camp. The guards told us that each family would have a house with electricity and running water—and that students like me would have access to education. As we closed our eyes to sleep, some of us began to get excited about the journey ahead. Some even made plans to buy audio cassettes to play in our new houses with electricity.

Three days later, immigration officers moved us via pick-up truck from Mpulungu to Kasama, the location of the government's regional offices. Again, we sheltered at a transit station.[5] Finally, on January 1, 1997, representatives of the Office of the United Nations High Commissioner for Refugees (UNHCR) escorted me and my fellow asylum seekers to a rail station for the trip to Kapiri Mposhi. Here, they transferred us to a bus bound for Meheba refugee settlement in Zambia's Northwestern Province, bordering Angola and Congo.

A SEVERE DISAPPOINTMENT

We arrived at Meheba Refugee Settlement in the middle of the night and were taken to sleep in a primary school along Road 36, the location of the camp administrative headquarters—where there was, in fact, electricity.

However, the very next morning some Congolese refugees already residing at Meheba came to see us. When they recognized that some of us had come to Meheba by way of Tanzania, they expressed dismay. "Why on earth have you come to Meheba where living conditions are so atrocious?" they asked, describing the camp's grass-thatched mud huts where rain could easily penetrate. Furthermore, they said, the stories

---

5   Locals told us that our Kasama shelter was an ex-prison used by the first Zambian President, David Kaunda, to lock up his enemies before feeding them to crocodiles in the nearby river.

we had heard of electricity in each refugee house had been a lie. We were shocked.

The current residents urged us not to allow UNHCR to transfer us out of Road 36. However, in a very short time UNHCR arrived at the primary school with three buses to move all of the recent arrivals, including our group of Burundians/Congolese, to Road 12, the location of a temporary group of huts designed to hold Angolan refugees waiting to be repatriated. The authorities assigned each couple a hut of their own, but singles had to share a hut with seven others.

In Road 12, I lived with six other guys—all from different backgrounds. I felt some comfort from the fact that I was the youngest and my roommates loved me as their brother. However, I was also extremely homesick. I had no idea where any of my family members were, because I had left Tanzania without news from Congo. Furthermore, most of the people living on Road 12 had connections to family abroad and expected to either join them or at least to receive money from them. I was the only one without a contact to whom I could write a letter.

At seventeen years old, I was away from family and had no news of what was happening either in Congo or in Burundi. I felt hopeless and depressed, not knowing what the future held for me. Many times when I went into the bush to get firewood, I would sit down and cry.

To learn more about my Zambian home away from home, read "Meheba Refugee Settlement" on *page 169.*

ANGRY AT GOD

During those early days at Meheba, I recalled my father's sad accounts of leaving behind his houses and businesses in Burundi. In exile, his faith had sustained him. Faith also played an important role in my life growing up in Congo, but I could not see the point of praying now. I alternated between thinking that God was punishing me for some unknown sin and being angry at him for not stopping the violence in my country.

Come to think of it, I probably did pray as I wrestled with these thoughts. My prayers took the form of accusations deep within my soul. *"Why couldn't you have chosen a Burundian president able to bring Hutu and Tutsi together, with full authority over all government departments?"* I asked, remembering the army's assassination of the man we had hoped would lead our nation to peace. Then, anticipating my ambitions in early adulthood, I added, *"Why could you not make me that kind of president?"* These silent prayers reflected my deep discouragement with all that my family and I had endured since fleeing the violence of 1972.

In his faithfulness and despite my anger, God gave me an idea that put an end to my sitting around, ruminating on my hopelessness. This idea soon developed into a profitable occupation.

UNHCR had made clear its intentions to move us out of Road 12 one by one, as more permanent accommodations with land to cultivate became available. But the Burundian/Congolese group I traveled with was adamant—we wanted to remain together, and since most of us were teachers or students, we had no desire to lead a life based on subsistence agriculture. We began dreaming of other businesses that could restore us to the standard of living to which we had become accustomed.

Each of us had been given a start pack by humanitarian aid workers. This start pack contained a blanket, two pots, a spoon and two plates. We pooled the contents of these packs, keeping three cooking pots and selling the rest to raise capital for our business ventures.

For my part, I sold my blanket and my cooking pot on the main road past the Meheba settlement, a two-hour walk from our sleeping quarters on Road 12. I found that others wanted to sell their pots and blankets, but did not want to walk a long distance or wait for buses to take them there. So they asked me to be their middleman, and I started going to the main road daily with their belongings. We agreed that I would sell each blanket for 7,000 Zambian Kwacha (ZK) to the public at the gates of the settlement—whereas, if we had sold a blanket to another refugee it would have brought only ZK4,000. At times I was able to sell a blanket for up to ZK12,000. When I took the money back to the owner, they would give me my ZK1,000 commission and would usually allow me to keep the extra profit I had negotiated.

I began praying what I would later admit was a very selfish prayer— that God would allow me to accumulate enough capital to start buying blankets directly from the refugees and selling them on the main road at a profit, not just for a commission. In my prayer, I vowed to God that I would give 10 percent of whatever profit I earned to the church. This became my business and my passion, and I soon accumulated the capital for which I had prayed.

In addition to selling on the main road, I also started selling within the refugee settlement to Zambian staff working in the hospital, in the schools, in the aid agencies, and in the police department. To generate a greater profit, I set aside a number of items for which I accepted payment in monthly installments for a higher cumulative price. I also discovered that refugees were not the only ones selling their blankets and pots. Some aid workers, after having distributed one starter kit per refugee, illegally sold the rest to generate some personal income.

Engaging in this kind of work not only resulted in financial rewards but in educational advancement as well. When I arrived at the Meheba settlement, I spoke no English. But since I sold to Angolans, Zambians, and others who spoke different languages, I had to learn a few words and phrases of English—a language used by all of my customers to one extent or another. Sometimes I would mix words from their native languages with English, and they laughed at me a lot.

In the evenings, I would ask my friend Ernest Musimbwa how to say in English the names and prices of the different items I had for sale. I would write those English words out pho-netically and memorize them at night for the next day's sales. In addition, I carried a pen and paper to write details of customers who took items on credit. I also wrote down the words I heard customers say so I could check their meaning with my friend in camp that night. This worked so well that one year after arriving in Meheba with no English, I was able to inquire about my case at the UNHCR office without needing a translator.

> *Meet Muchaila, a resident of Meheba camp, whose resilience and initiative has made him a success. Read "The Master Mechanic" on page 171.*

LEARNING TO WORK TOGETHER

Soon I had accumulated capital of ZK65,000, but I had not given any money to the church.

Eventually, Meheba's administration relented and agreed to give our entire group of Burundians and Congolese some ground along Road 18 on which we could build several mud houses. They even dug us a new well, so we wouldn't have to draw water from the wells of our Angolan neighbors.

I and a few others in our group decided to form a joint venture. We would hire trucks to transport sweet potatoes grown by the Angolans and sell them in Solwezi, Chingola, and Kitwe—major population centers along the copper belt in Zambia. We loaded over 400 bags of sweet potatoes on the first truck we hired. Unfortunately, the truck blew a tire before it left camp. Getting a spare tire to replace the ruined one took hours. Finally, we could continue our journey to Chingola, about 250 kilometers distant, but we had traveled less than 75 kilometers when the truck broke down again. Two days later, we finally arrived in Chingola where we again had to wait—this time for another group of entrepreneurs to finish selling their potatoes. Then we could begin selling ours.

All hope of making lots of money evaporated as we discovered almost half our cargo of sweet potatoes had spoiled due to the delays on the road. We sold the rest, and after paying the owner of the truck, we had less than half our initial capital.

Discouraged, some of the partners suggested we end our joint venture then and there, but others held onto the hope of making a profit. Obviously this business had potential. We bought a bag of sweet potatoes from the Angolans at ZK500 and paid less than ZK200 a bag for the transport, while bags of sweet potatoes retailed from ZK1,500 to ZK3,500, depending on their quality and the quantity of potatoes on the market. After much deliberation, we agreed to continue our joint venture but to be careful in the future to hire good trucks.

At that point I remembered I had vowed before God to give 10 percent of my income to the church—but I still had not kept my promise. This time, I prayed to God asking him to forgive me and to make our business succeed, adding, "I will certainly carry out my vow."

PERFECTING OUR JOINT VENTURE

The second truck we hired hauled our goods to Chingola without any breakdowns, but when we arrived we discovered many other truckloads of sweet potatoes flooding the market. In spite of the competition, we managed to sell everything, and we made a small profit.

On our next attempt, we hired a much larger truck—able to carry 1,500 bags of potatoes. The driver had just finished unloading goods in Solwezi and wanted to return as soon as possible to Lusaka (Zambia's capital city) so we were able to hire him at a bargain price. We took him to the Meheba settlement to load the sweet potatoes. Although we did not have enough capital to buy an entire truckload, we managed to get some potatoes on credit. It was a fast game; we worked day and night to get 1,000 bags ready.

This time, we drove to Kitwe, Zambia, about 50 kilometers beyond Chingola. To our delight, we were the only sweet potato truck in that city's marketplace. People flocked to us.

In order to handle the demand, we divided our responsibilities: two of us stayed in the truck giving out bags to whoever had paid. Two others collected money, one recorded the sales and a few others watched for thieves. The most trustworthy man in our group, the one designated our leader and treasurer, held all of our money. Whenever we sold a bag, we brought the money to him.

At one point, we could no longer control the crowd. This forced a change in our strategy. We all became salesmen, entrusting the money to our treasurer.

We finished selling our truckload of sweet potatoes in about four hours. Although thieves took a few bags by force, we knew that we had made a large profit because we sold each bag of sweet potatoes between ZK1,500 and ZK3,500. Exhausted from our manual labor, we all went to eat and lay down. No one bothered to count the money.

EMBEZZLEMENT SOURS SUCCESS

When it came time to divide up the profits, we received an unpleasant surprise. Disbelief followed shock as the man holding all of our money tried to persuade us that a portion of our profits had been stolen from him. The money he distributed to each of us amounted to less than half of what we expected.

Most of us stood speechless, but some of our cohort appeared to believe that the money could have been taken by thieves during the sale. With all the crowds and commotion, and since no one bothered to count the money after we concluded business, it seemed impossible to tell what had happened. However, some of us suspected our treasurer of deceiving us, because those who supported his story came from his extended family.

After much discussion, the man agreed to pay back a certain amount of the money to cover the loss, but that still left us wondering how the money had vanished. Some of the partners suggested taking the issue to the police in Kitwe. In the end, we agreed to keep our integrity and to seek the counsel of the leaders in our refugee community—Congolese from South Kivu. Returning to the Meheba Camp, we asked our community leaders to help, but nothing significant came of it.

This failure of a trusted business partner revived my sorrows, because I immediately remembered the lack of trust I displayed toward God by failing to honor my promise to tithe. When things went right for me, I had totally forgotten my vow to give 10 percent to the church. When things went wrong, I had cried out for mercy and increased my commitment—only to forget my commitment on the upswing. I felt like such a liar, and I begged God to forgive me.

Though penitent, I still did not think of tithing, even on the ZK30,000 I had left from my ZK65,000 investment in the sweet potato business. I looked at my dwindling profits as a very small amount from which a gift of 10 percent would be insignificant.

GIVING IT ANOTHER TRY

Those involved in our failed sweet potato venture included Dizo Kajolo, with his two brothers and a colleague, Issa Saddy. I viewed Dizo and Issa as good friends and dedicated Christians, even with the hard times we had just experienced. The five of us pooled what money we had left and sent Issa to buy fish. By reducing the number of partners I still trusted, I hoped to earn a good profit. My hope turned to gloom when Issa returned with bad news. Without any visa or valid form of identification, he narrowly escaped imprisonment when crossing the Zambia/Congo border to buy fish. He did, however, manage to bring back a small amount of fish which I sold in the camp. From my ZK30,000 investment, I recovered only ZK15,000.

This time, I projected all the blame onto God. I accused him of not hearing my prayers and of not paying attention to an orphan, which I considered myself as I still had no news about my family. Years later, I realized that God had remained faithful to me, in the face of my unfaithfulness and accusation. All along, he had been teaching me valuable lessons about trusting others and about my lack of trust in his sufficiency. Even though I wasn't a quick learner, he knew exactly what he was doing.

At this point, God showed his faithfulness in the form of a friend named Bonne-Année Rugoyera. I was trying to resume my former business of selling blankets, pots, spoons, and plates when Bonne-Année asked if we could share the profits in a combined business, which would use his money as capital. I agreed, and he gave me ZK80,000. His generosity stirred a conflict within me. On the one hand, I felt great joy at being entrusted with a significant amount of money to start a business. On the other hand, I worried because of my failures in previous business ventures. Yet, I believed that God intended to bless me at this point—so I pressed on.

Everything I bought with my personal money I sold for credit, which resulted in greater profit because of the interest charged—whereas, I used my friend's capital for fast cash sales. Within a period of four months, I had returned to Bonne-Année his capital and had earned a sizable profit.

I had worked tirelessly to sell our housewares in and out of the camp, frequently walking long distances and carrying heavy loads. I felt like resting for a while before embarking on my next venture.

That's when I received a message from UNHCR—they wanted to send me to Tanzania.

REBIRTH OF HOPE

This news stemmed from a process I had set in motion one year earlier, soon after my arrival at Meheba. I had lied to UNHCR by claiming Rev. Samuel and Magdalene Bazira as my father and mother and by telling the authorities that my family had been spotted in Kigoma, Tanzania. Refugees often lie to get out of difficult situations, and I never felt guilty about the deception. With this lie, I hoped to get away from the Zambian refugee settlement, which at first appearance had been less than I expected.[6]

Meanwhile, the processing of my claim, though it took some time to work out, had continued throughout the past twelve months. UNHCR had apparently verified Rev. Bazira's whereabouts and had approved transport money for me to join my *adoptive* family in Tanzania.

Summoned to UNHCR's offices at Meheba, I received an envelope

---

6   Though I did not continue my schooling at Meheba, as I had hoped, I did learn a great deal about business here.

containing ZK40,000 plus US$50, along with a travel permit signed by the Zambian government. It would be an understatement to say "I was a happy young man."

About the same time, I received a letter from my cousin Vincent—the first communication I had had with my *real* family since leaving Congo. The letter stated that my brother Josaphat's wife Cizanye had attempted to flee to Tanzania but had drowned in Lake Tanganyika along with other members of our Kenya-Tanganyika community.

However, my brothers Josaphat and Hari and my sister Miriam all made it safely to Mtabila Refugee Camp in Tanzania. Vincent's letter also informed me that my mother, Guenèse, had returned to Burundi with her second husband and that my dad, who had also returned to Burundi, had married for the third time. Vincent concluded the letter with these words, "If you have no chance of studying in Zambia, please come over to Tanzania."

For the full account of this tragic story, turn to "Lost beneath the Waves" on page 173.

Some refugees, like me, left Meheba Refugee Settlement willingly. Some were forced to leave after standing up for their rights. Read the story of "A Refugee Advocate" on page 177.

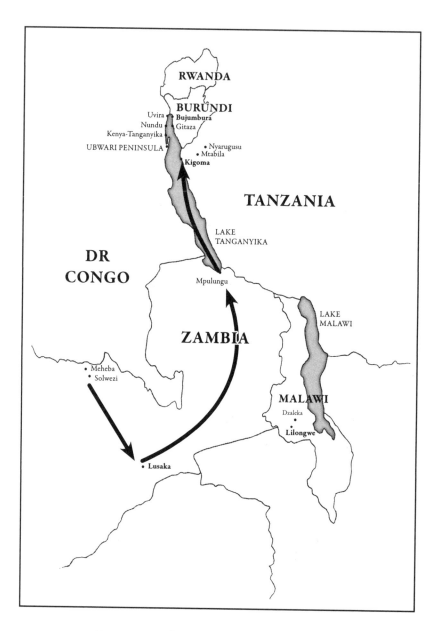

Innocent's Journey at Age 18

CHAPTER 5

Swindled

In March 1998, I walked through the gates of Meheba refugee settlement for the last time as a refugee, but I did not immediately leave Zambia. I had never been to the capital city of any country, so I made my way to Lusaka, Zambia. My main goal was to have someone take a photo of me with some high-rise buildings in the background. I intended to show the photo to people in the Tanzanian refugee camps, bragging that I had traveled widely.

While in Lusaka, I stayed with friends who owned a small shop in Old Kanyama. In this crowded, low-income part of the city, refugees who no longer lived in camps could afford to rent tiny shanties with windows facing a public path. These shanties served both as sleeping rooms and as tiny shops where refugees could earn a living providing almost anything their neighbors might need.

Feeling very rich with the money I had in my pockets, I paid for the bus fares for my friends as they showed me the sights of Lusaka. While sightseeing, I reported to the UNHCR office there. They wanted to hold my transport money for me, but I refused, believing I was clever enough to hide it from potential thieves. Secretly, I thought that if I let them put my money in their safe, I would not get it back. Though I did not know it then, I exhibited the character of a typical refugee in that I had difficulty trusting people outside my tribe or close circle of friends—even those trying to help me.

On March 19, UNHCR took me to Lusaka's central hospital to be vaccinated for yellow fever, and the medical personnel told me to wait for ten days before traveling. During this time, I bought new clothes, shoes, a camera, and a few other things. At the end of the ten days, I got my bag ready for travel and planned to stop one last time at the UNHCR office to announce my departure. With that notice, they would inform their Tanzanian office that I was coming.

I had dressed up for the occasion of this big trip. For security purposes, I divided my travel money into four parcels and stashed it on various parts of my body. The money I needed to travel from Lusaka to Mpulungu[1] was in the pocket of my shorts, under my trousers. I hid the US$50 note and ZK140,000 in two envelopes, inside my socks. Finally, I put ZK10,000 in the right pocket of my trousers for drinks and meals.

Then, I boarded a bus from Old Kanyama to the center of Lusaka

---

1   Mpulungu—A port in northeastern Zambia on the south end of Lake Tanganyika. I arrived in Zambia at this port in 1996, and I left Zambia at this port in 1998.

where I disembarked and began walking toward the Intercity Bus Terminal. Once there, I intended to buy a ticket for a bus going to Mpulungu. I marveled at the contrast between the tall, modern office buildings and the street vendors plying their wares at the foundations of these buildings. A mixture of car and pedestrian traffic clogged the streets between 9:00 a.m. and noon.

As I walked down a street named Freedom Way, a man dressed as a rural official rushed to talk with me. A second man accompanied him. The first man addressed me in Chibemba, the most widely spoken language in Zambia, but I asked him to speak in English.

"I am from a village and have come to withdraw money from a bank to pay my employees who teach primary school," he began. "But I am fearful to ask anyone to help because they may steal the money."

"When I saw you, I had a strong conviction that you would be able to help," he continued. "Please watch my car as I get the money."

"It will not take long," he concluded. "The bank is near, and I will pay you right away for your assistance." I accepted without questioning his story.

He pointed to one of the nicer automobiles in a parking lot. "This is my car," he said. "Just stay here and watch so that no one breaks in." He added, "My friend and I will bring the money from the bank."

Before leaving, the man had one more request. "Would you show us how much money you have?" he said. "I need to be assured that you will not steal from us." I protested that I was a Christian and did not steal from anyone. As I spoke these words, I was removing my money from the locations where I had hidden it.

The man's friend gave me a large envelope to keep all of my money in. "Keep everything in one place," he advised me. "That way, when we return, it will be easier for us to search you to see if you have stolen anything from the car." Naively, I put all my money into the envelope. After counting it, the men gave the envelope back to me, and I slid it into my left sock under my trousers. I tried giving them my bag also, to assure them I was trustworthy, but they refused. "Keep the bag with you," said the man. "We believe you."

The man and his friend paid me ZK5,000 as an advance and promised to give me more afterwards. Then, they walked down the street as I stood watching their car.

After waiting about twenty minutes, I began to wonder why the man and his friend were not bringing boxes of money from the bank. I began searching for them in order to give back the advance, since I could wait no longer. I asked someone on the street and was told there was no bank nearby. I was advised to walk away, but my conscience would not allow me to leave Freedom Way without giving back their money.

That's when I decided to get my money out of the large envelope which the man and his friend had given me. My heart sank when I discovered there was no money inside it—only newspaper. I had been swindled.

In a state of shock, I reported to the UNHCR office. Officials there offered only one solution: return to Meheba Refugee Settlement and wait for another opportunity to travel to Tanzania, but they would not guarantee that would happen.

Still reeling from being robbed, I accused God of abandoning me. If He still loved me, He would not have allowed these men to steal my money, I reasoned.

God had not abandoned me

Not wanting to go back to Meheba, I remained in Lusaka without a flicker of hope. Then, two days later, a friend named Emmanuel heard of my plight. A fellow Burundian refugee, Emmanuel had left the settlement a few months before me and, despite his legal status as a refugee, had found work in Lusaka.

While living in Meheba, Emmanuel had amassed enormous debts and many of his creditors harassed him to the point of forcibly removing articles of clothing from him whenever they saw him. He owed me money as well, but I never harassed him, even when I really needed the money.

Remembering this, Emmanuel came to where I stayed in Lusaka and asked what kind of help I needed. He took me to his house and fed me for almost two weeks, looking for a way to get me to Mpulungu and promising to pay my fare by ship to Tanzania.

At length, Emmanuel introduced me to another Burundian who worked for the Sable Transport Company in Lusaka. This man arranged for me to ride in a company truck from Lusaka to Mpulungu. At Mpulungu, I spent three days and nights in the immigration office waiting for a ship to Kigoma, Tanzania.

When the ship arrived, I marshalled all my courage and got on board, ignoring the consequences of not having a ticket. Fed up with the city in which I had been swindled, I had left Lusaka before Emmanuel could give me fare money for the ship. As a result, I did not know where the money for my trip to Kigoma would come from.

I hoped the Zambian immigration officers would help me get to

Kigoma free of charge, but they did not. When I was told about their refusal, I bought a very cheap ticket to take me out of Zambia (but not a full ticket to Kigoma) because I was frightened the immigration officers would send me back to Meheba.

While waiting for the ship to get underway, a passenger encouraged me to approach a well-known Tanzanian Ministry of Transportation official in charge of on-board ticket sales. I drew a deep breath and took the risk. To my surprise, when I approached the official, he waved me over.

"Innocent, how are you?" he said. I was surprised when I heard him speak my name, so I quickly presented my request.

"As you passed the Zambian Immigration officers, I saw you and heard of your problem," said the official. "I will try to help you."

"After all," he added, "Burundians and Tanzanians are one."

I felt reassured and thanked the official profusely for his kind help. He even asked if I needed further assistance. "No," I replied, though in fact I had no money for food on the voyage. I felt unworthy to receive any more help from this man, since I had already received the most important favor.

The next day, I arrived in Kigoma, Tanzania where I reported to the office of UNHCR and was taken to Mtabila Refugee Camp, about 100 kilometers (62 miles) northeast of this major city in western Tanzania and just a few kilometers east of my home country, Burundi.

REUNION WITH FAMILY

My brothers, my sister, and other relatives in Mtabila Refugee Camp had heard that I would come, but they had no idea of the actual day. I arrived when no one expected me, and it proved to be a good surprise—full of laughter and tears. As my brother Hari enfolded me in his strong arms, I reflected on the struggles I endured alone in Zambia. At last I felt secure.

After everyone had hugged me, I took a shower and ate a late lunch prepared especially for me. Evening came, and when I finished answering everyone's questions about my survival in Zambia, they allowed me to ask about what happened following my departure from Congo. The stories they told of death and persecution of Burundian refugees during the civil war overwhelmed me.

Eventually, my family informed me that Mum had been killed by soldiers during an attack in Burundi.[2] She died while I was in Zambia, but no one wanted to tell me the sad news in a letter. They thought I would be upset without any family member to comfort me. They were right.

It took several days for me to accept Mum's death. Whenever I saw my sister Miriam, I cried because her thin nose, the lightness of her skin, her mouth, and her general appearance reminded me of my mother. Some of my relatives and friends, who knew the story of my parents' divorce, wondered why I mourned for my mother so many years after she had left me as a toddler. They never understood how much I loved Mum and what I planned to do for her once I had an education and became a success.

PREPARING FOR SCHOOL

All of my dreams and future prospects depended upon the level of education I could attain. This thought had been engrained in my thinking

---

2   I later learned that Mum died of malnutrition, not at the hands of soldiers.

over the years by my family and all who had cared for me. For this reason, I decided to continue my studies at Nyarugusu, a camp for Congolese refugees located two or three hours by foot from Mtabila.

I would attend school with Déo, the son of my cousin Magdalene and Pastor Samuel Bazira. The Baziras had cared for my family in Congo, during my father's extended absence. They later moved to Kigoma, where they sheltered me in 1996 as I fled the Congolese civil war. Now, they lived in Mtabila Refugee Camp.

When the war broke out in Congo, it had interrupted my third year of secondary school (ninth grade). This time I knew the importance of school, so I wanted to attend and excel without the need of my family's encouragement.

Déo, on the other hand, had failed the sixth grade three times. He was about to give up, when I suggested the idea of taking him with me. His parents doubted Déo's chances of improvement, but they finally allowed their son to accompany me to Nyarugusu. Deo promised to be obedient and listen to me while we were away from home.

In Nyarugusu, we would stay with Rev. Jonas Ngabwe, who had been a Free Methodist pastor in Nundu, Congo where I was born. Rev. Ngabwe knew both my father and Rev. Bazira. The Ngabwes had eleven children and many grandchildren. They sacrificed greatly to accommodate us, and gave Déo and me much love and support.

As I prepared for school, I was determined to spend as much time and attention as possible on school matters so that the goals I had for my life would have a chance of becoming reality. I knew I had not done well in chemistry, physics, and mathematics in the past, but I was determined to succeed at this new school.

One means of preparation involved visiting a witchdoctor who a friend told me sold potions that could increase the capacity of my memory. My friend told of other students who had used these potions and what amazing results they had achieved. Since his suggestion was in support of my education, and I knew I was not gifted in the sciences, I decided to go for it. However, I told none of my family members since I was ashamed of the conflict between relying on this source of power and my Christian faith.

The witchdoctor and his wife could not read or write; neither could their children. It never occurred to me to ask why he would sell the remedy to others while neglecting his own family. After I paid him, the witchdoctor took a used razor and made two small cuts on my head. I did not think about the thousands of Africans who had been infected with HIV due to unclean razors and knives used in these practices.

Next, the witchdoctor pressed a mixture of dried herbs into the cuts and gave me two other small packages of herbs. He told me to mix the first packet with water and dust picked up from a crossroads at dawn. He instructed me to wrap the second packet of herbs in a piece of paper and smoke it on the day before any test. Doing this, said the witchdoctor, would enable me to remember everything I had learned at school, but it would only work in combination with the first packet and the tattoos on my head.

Despite dabbling with these potions, I did grow in my relationship with God. In August, one month prior to the beginning of school, I decided to sell the camera I bought in Zambia. I had been using it to take photos of people for profit. But I had made little money with it, compared to others who seemed to be earning a good living from their photography.

While waiting for a buyer to bring money for my camera, I lay on my bed planning how I would invest the money to help me through school. This revived old memories of the losses I experienced in business in Zambia, and I sensed that the money from the camera would yield no profit either. I concluded that the reason for my past financial failures stemmed from my repeated failure to give 10 percent of my income to the church, as I had promised God.

Realizing that I was the obstacle to my own progress, I got up from my bed and began sobbing deeply.

Quickly, I sought out Mrs. Bazira, who had played a mother's role in my life growing up in Congo. I told her of my predicament and asked her to keep all the money I received from the camera until I gave 10 percent to my local church.

After giving my tithe, I cannot describe the great peace I felt in my heart. The fear of business failure vanished instantaneously. I was once again eager to invest and confident of making a good return.

I asked my cousin Mwavita, who was going to Dar es Salaam in eastern Tanzania, to buy some second-hand goods. She brought back some shoes and watches which I sold at the camp. When re-invested, the money earned with this initial capital lasted me from the fall of 1998, when I left for school in Nyarugusu, until 2003.[3]

---

3   Though successful in business again, I realized that God's blessing had never left me. I would certainly not suggest that financial prosperity always means God's blessing or that poverty is a curse.

Chapter 6

Learning to Lead

School at Nyarugusu Refugee Camp in Tanzania opened the first week of September of 1998. Early in the year, I ranked among the three top students in the ninth grade while Déo led the other students in seventh grade.

Despite the success I achieved by hard work, I still wondered if I could do better by using the potion I had purchased. One day, I put the potion to a test. A chemistry exam had been scheduled for the following day. Instead of studying, I stayed up late with friends.

Next morning, I arose and went to the bathroom with my *medicine* and matches. As instructed by the witchdoctor, I wrapped part of the potion in a piece of paper and smoked it while repeating these words: "Remind me what the teacher taught in class. I want to be the highest."

Then I sat for the exam and waited expectantly for the potion to work its magic. It didn't.

I was so disappointed that I threw the rest of the potion into the toilet and never told anyone about this misadventure.

ORGANIZING MY CLASSMATES

While studying at Nyarugusu, I helped to organize a union of Burundian students who, like me, had come from Mtabila Refugee Camp.

Burundians chose to study in this camp for Congolese refugees for many reasons. Many of us had been raised and educated in Congo, so we felt at home in the environment at Nyarugusu. At the same time, we sought peace of mind and body since the politically charged atmosphere in Mtabila could erupt in conflict at any moment. Finally, the Congolese government sent examination papers to their students in Tanzania. Therefore, studying in a camp for Congolese refugees assured us of receiving an internationally recognized certificate superior to the secondary school certificate provided by UNHCR at Mtabila.

Since the majority of Burundian students had been born in Congo, the Congolese refugees tolerated us. However, the government of Tanzania had separated refugees according to their nationality, and it was illegal for Burundians to be found in the Congolese camp. The Burundian students lived in fear of being deported. They hid their nationality and spoke the Congolese dialects to avoid discovery.

I was not happy with the idea of hiding my nationality—my identity. So, I gathered a small number of like-minded students into a Burundian Student Club that would challenge every Burundian student to accept who he or she was. Club members elected two older students to the positions of president and vice president. They elected me, a ninth grader, as secretary.

It wasn't easy to recruit other students at first, but after a while, many overcame their fear and joined. The members met twice a month to encourage each other to study and maintain high moral standards, to share portions of the Bible that were meaningful to us, to help each other in times of need, and to further our personal relationships.

The Burundian Student Club fostered an atmosphere of accountability among the Burundian students. Even our relatives in Mtabila Refugee Camp came to know and trust each other to carry food or gift parcels to their children at Nyarugusu.

Faith becomes real

After completing the first semester at Nyarugusu, Deo and I returned to Mtabila for the holidays and proudly reported our successes in the classroom. Deo, who had previously been considered a total failure, now ranked the highest in his seventh grade class and in the entire school. I ranked fourth highest in my ninth grade class.

To understand how "Music Releases Pain, Recharges Hope" in a refugee camp, turn to page 179.

Despite our achievements, a series of questions haunted me. Why did neighbors continue to kill neighbors in Burundi, where civil war had raged on since 1993? I knew God to be all powerful, but did he not have sufficient love to establish peace in my motherland? More personally—was I destined to live in one refugee camp after another until I died?

Previously, whenever these kinds of questions arose, I would become pensive and withdraw from friends and family for two or three days. The only thing that could pacify my mind and heart was singing.

This time, however, I could not bear the intensity of these troubling questions.

Adding to my sorrow, I received a letter from my father in Burundi. In the letter, he described his struggles to find shelter and food while watching his houses and farms being occupied and exploited by others. With his frequent illnesses, I feared Dad would die before I got a chance to see him again. I asked if I could pay him a visit, but he refused. "Burundi is still a dangerous place," he explained.

With all this weighing on my heart and mind, I visited a prayer group affiliated with the Free Methodist Church in Mtabila which was well-known for miraculous healings. The aim of my visit was to receive prayer for emotional burdens which had become too great for me to bear. I joined a long queue of people waiting to get in.

The first step was to meet with a counselor who would lead me through a time of reflection and confession. When my turn came, I prepared to confess my doubt about God's love for my family, for the nation of Burundi, and for Africa as a whole. To my surprise, before I said anything, the woman who counseled me began to pray. As she prayed, God revealed to her much of what was on my heart as well as things she could not have known about me.

For example, the counselor reminded me of dreams I had had— dreams that I had not shared with anyone—and she explained their meaning. I wept with joy as I realized that the God I had accused of inflicting misery upon us had, in fact, great and wonderful plans for my life—plans not to harm me but to give me hope and a future.

Now at twenty-one years of age, this experience transformed my life. I vowed to trust God in everything from that day forward and to dedicate my life to following the teachings of Jesus. This vow may sound strange to some, since I had already been baptized as a teenager. But the earlier event was a formality, to meet the wishes of my father. This was a personal decision.

MY FEAR OF HIV

In 2000, while on holiday at Mtabila camp, I decided to donate blood. A relative had emergency surgery during childbirth and needed blood, so I went to the hospital with the intention of helping her. First, a medical assistant took a sample from my arm and tested it. Then, after checking the results, a nurse began to draw blood.

She had almost finished when a second medical assistant walked in the room. His expression darkened as he rechecked my test results, and I knew something must be wrong. He called the person who had performed the test on my blood, and they both went outside to look at it in the sunlight. They also looked at it under a microscope.

Finally, the second assistant told a doctor, "It is not safe."

During all of this, I pretended to be unaware of what was happening. Yet, I closely followed every action and every word. When the assistant pronounced my blood unsafe and marked it with a red pen, I concluded that I must be HIV positive. No one told me otherwise, and I was too afraid to ask for confirmation.

Returning home, I became despondent. I asked myself when and where I could have caught the virus. One event came to mind. I had attempted sex just once, a few months before my baptism.

In 1994 at age fifteen, I found myself surrounded by peers who practiced sex with multiple partners. I felt inadequate when they shared stories of their sexual experiences while I just listened. Bowing to pressure, I took a step to prove to myself and to my friends that I was a man. I arranged to meet a girlfriend after dark.

I was curious to know how it felt to sleep with a woman. On the other hand, I feared being caught as I was considered a model young man. The parents of all my friends admired me.

I was torn. But since I wanted to be on the same wavelength as my friends, I stuck with my plan to explore sex with my girlfriend. Before leaving home that night, I knelt and prayed along these lines: "God, forgive me. I am going to sin. I have heard stories from my friends about sex. I want to try. I need to try so I can have something to say to the others."

At my baptism a few months later, my father told me I was repenting of all the mistakes I had made. He said that God would forgive me and give me a fresh start. He also asked me not to have sex until I got married. "If you do have sex," he added, "I would rather pay the dowry for the girl so that, when you come of age, you will get married and not have any other sexual partners." These heavy words and the grace of God helped me to abstain from sex after my baptism.

Now, six years later, I wondered if I had really been infected in that single sexual attempt—or perhaps by the witchdoctor's dirty razor. My diet had certainly been poor over the last six years, and my living conditions were far from healthy, yet I had no visible symptoms of HIV. I wondered why God would protect me from wars but did not protect me from this infection. In my hopelessness and despair, I thought of the many times since my baptism when I had said no to sex, and now I regretted having missed out—all for nothing.

Despite this internal conflict, I did not share my troubled heart with anyone. If I had shown any sadness, they would have suspected a negative result from the hospital. I chose to suffer alone, in part because of the stigma HIV carried in the Christian community. At the time, people believed only sinners could be infected with HIV.

It had been one year since I rededicated my life to Jesus Christ. I had left behind all of my pain and disappointment and had trusted that God would bring about his good purpose in my life. But now that I thought I was HIV positive, I fell back into self-pity because my community of faith regarded HIV as God's punishment for sin.

For an entire week after my hospital visit, I did not want to be alone. Fear consumed me, and I thought constantly of death. During the day, I tried to look strong, but when night came, I could not sleep. Two voices battled inside of me. One said, *"Since you are HIV positive, go ahead and sleep around, for nothing good remains in you."* The second, quieter voice said, *"Remember that no matter what, you are still a Christian whose home is in heaven."*

The quieter voice prevailed. In His mercy, God reminded me deep within my spirit of the promises he had for my life. I still worried, but as the days passed, my faith grew stronger. I began to pray for healing. I even wrote a letter to a Christian organization based in Nairobi, Kenya, asking for their prayers. They wrote back, encouraging me with these words. "God said your name is engraved in the palms of His hands. He will do exceedingly abundantly above all which you ask or think."

I soon realized that by spending time praying, reading the Bible, and fasting, I would gain more spiritual strength to trust God for healing. I began to set aside time for regular prayer, and I fasted three days of every

Meet a Nyarugusu teacher focused on returning home and "Making Congo Better," on page 181.

month. I composed many songs during this time and became more active in the church, doing everything with dedication and passion. I also taught during youth services in Nyarugusu Refugee Camp and realized my giftedness in teaching and preaching.

PLEADING OUR CASE

I remember the 2001-02 school year as a remarkable milestone in my academic life. At the end of my senior year, I anticipated graduating from *Institut Pedagogique de L'Amitié* in Nyarugusu[1] after which I would be qualified to teach primary school.

Then one night, gunshots rang out and rumors spread that armed Burundians had tried to steal goods from this Congolese refugee camp.[2]

Next day, the camp authorities enacted sanctions meant to protect residents from further violence. Among these sanctions, the authorities announced that all Burundian students must return to their own camps

---

1   Institut Pedagogique de L'Amitié–Friendship Teacher Training College, one of two French-speaking high schools operating in Nyarugusu when I attended classes there.

2   Actually, refugees in Nyarugusu had purchased cows from rebel groups near the Burundian border. Two armed men came to camp to get their money. When security guards tried to arrest them, the rebels fired two bullets in the air.

immediately. They also changed the monthly school fee system so that Burundian students had to pay double the fees of Congolese students. Some Burundian students started paying the higher fees immediately while others packed their bags to go home.

I decided to challenge the decision of the authorities. Because the other officers had already graduated, only I remained as a leader of the Burundian Student Club. I searched both high schools in the camp, looking for others willing to explore ways of stopping the discrimination against Burundian students. I found three other Burundian seniors determined to take on this challenge.

As we considered various strategies, some of our fellow Burundian students tried to discourage us. "You will anger the Congolese if you oppose them," they said. "We should just pay the higher fees and keep quiet."

I had to admit that any opposition to the new rules carried with it a degree of risk. But then I remembered a dream one of my classmates had before the beginning of the year. In the dream he saw me writing the Congolese national exams. Recalling that dream, I knew God intended for me to complete my high school in the Congolese refugee camp.

Finally, the four of us came up with a plan. We would plead our case in a letter to the stakeholders of education in the camp. The letter would be addressed to the committee of parents acting as educational advisors, with copies sent to the education coordinator, to the leader of the entire Congolese community and his staff, and to the headmasters of both high schools.

We spent all of Sunday evening, December 9, 2001, gathering persuasive facts and writing the letter. In this written appeal, we praised the Congolese community for accepting Burundian students without discrimination from the start. We talked about the bond shared by

Congolese and Burundian refugees, both forced to flee their countries. We stressed our common ancestry as part of the Bantu family of tribes, and we emphasized the high value of the education offered at Nyaragusu. Finally, we pointed to the limited financial means of the Burundian students facing the fee increase and the fact that some students were already packing to return home.

The letter concluded:

"We beg you to show once more the spirit of hospitality and patriotism to soothe the wounds of this miserable existence of ours, wounds that will follow us to the grave. We beg you to address this problem that is consuming us, because—as you have been teaching us in civic education—much can be achieved by hatred but more can be achieved by love."

As previously agreed upon, we distributed copies of this three-page handwritten letter to every individual and office before 10:00 a.m. the following morning. We told the Burundian students to watch for any reaction: positive or negative. Then we waited.

To our surprise, all of the individuals and offices to which we sent the letter gathered for an immediate meeting to discuss the matter, and they decided in our favor! It was exciting to be approached by these leaders who congratulated us for a wise and convincing tactic.

The officials rolled back the school fee increase for Burundian students and told students who had already paid the inflated fees that their payment would cover two months instead of one.

FINISHING WELL

After this exhilarating conclusion to our crisis, I felt God's approval and trusted Him more and more. The experience reinvigorated my desire to bring my secondary school education to a successful conclusion.

As the Congolese national exams approached, a handful of classmates and I organized study groups to prepare for them. The study groups met at school every evening from 8:00 p.m. until 11:00 p.m. to review information we would be expected to know for the exams. We went to sleep at school and woke up at 2:00 a.m. for more review. At 4:00 a.m., we would go home, shower, and have breakfast before coming back to school.

One night, I found myself alone at school. My friends were either at home or otherwise occupied. I studied a bit and then spent some time praying. I lay down to sleep and that is when I had an extraordinary spiritual experience I can only call "a visit from God."

I felt shivers coming from my toes slowly up the rest of my body until they covered my hair. My whole body quivered uncontrollably. I wondered what to make of this. After a while, I rose to my feet and began praying again, thanking God for whatever he had done in my body.

At first, I thought he had healed me from HIV, but I still didn't have the courage to be tested for the infection.[3]

A week later, I sat with my classmates for the national exams.

---

3   Not until 2007, when I fell in love with the woman who would later become my wife, did I gather the courage to be tested for HIV. I did not have the virus and felt stupid for living in fear for so long.

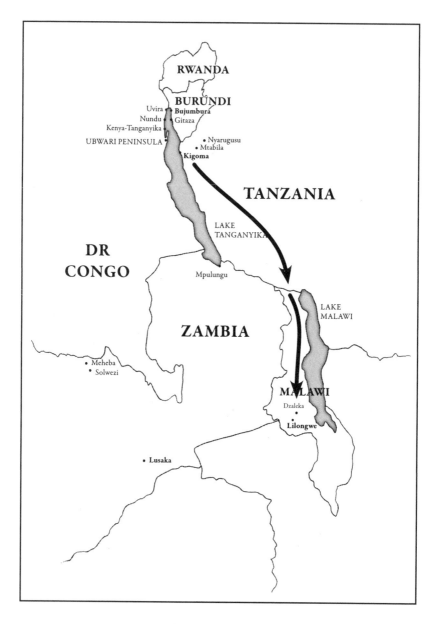

Innocent's Journey at Age 24

CHAPTER 7

Bound for Malawi

While I sat for the national exams at Nyarugusu, my father died. Dad passed away in his beloved Burundi, after struggling for years with stress and mental instability from watching all that he had accomplished as a young man be destroyed by the constant conflict between Hutu rebels and Tutsi soldiers. Our family's village became a frequent battlefield throughout Burundi's civil war, which lasted from 1993 to 2005.

With others occupying his properties and with his children all living in refugee camps, Dad could no longer hold onto life. He had lost all hope.

A Burundian radio station, monitored by our refugee community in the Tanzanian camps, announced my father's death just two days after his passing. In Burundi, due to the cost and unreliability of the telephone network, families often chose to place a public announcement on the radio to communicate the death of a family member. Nobody in the refugee camps had phones at the time.

News of Dad's passing disappointed but did not surprise me. Two months before his death, Dad sent me a letter wishing me success in my exams. In the letter he commended me for continuing my education and renewing my Christian faith. He also encouraged me to take care of the family because, of all my siblings, only I had continued in school with the potential of attaining a higher level of education and eventual employment.

At the end of the letter, Dad asked me not to worry about him. He admitted that life hadn't been easy but said that God's love sustained him. The letter read like a father giving his blessing to the son he loves, knowing that time is short.

Dad's death disappointed me because I loved him very much and planned to help him forget all his misery by taking care of him in his old age. I imagined myself building a good house for him, driving him places, and meeting his basic needs.

Now, just as I had achieved a measure of success in my life, Dad was gone.

*   *   *

After finishing my exams, I returned to Mtabila Refugee Camp to look for work. I had great confidence that I could land a job. My negotiations on behalf of the Burundian students in Nyarugusu had made me something of a hero in this neighboring camp.

In March 2003, Mtabila's school system hired me as a substitute teacher for grades three, four, and five. The job proved challenging because I had little experience with the Burundian education system—only what I had observed during my family's brief return to our country in 1993. I had spent the rest of my school days in the Congolese system.

The fifth grade students quickly gave me the nickname "Mon Dieu" which simply means "My God." I got this nickname because whenever a student failed to answer my question, I exclaimed "Mon Dieu!"

One month later, the school administrators assigned me as a permanent teacher to the third grade. I taught from 7:00 a.m. to 5:00 p.m. with an hour off midday, Monday through Friday. All of my time and effort earned a salary of less than US$20 per month. Though overworked and underpaid, I enjoyed teaching my students and fellow Burundians.

ON THE MOVE AGAIN

Despite my satisfaction with teaching and the comfort of being near family, restlessness dogged my soul. Most refugees my age languished in Mtabila with little prospect of getting out. On the other hand, Emile Niyonzima, my friend with whom I organized the Burundian Student Club in Nyarugusu, had traveled to Malawi. At Dzaleka Refugee Camp he had won a scholarship to study and settle in Canada.

Besides, my 1994 run-in with the Tutsi army continued to haunt me. Though protected by UNHCR and the government of Tanzania, Mtabila Refugee Camp remained politically unstable. Its proximity to the border with Burundi made it vulnerable to frequent attacks by rebel groups and thieves.

In search of greater opportunity but also for my own security, I decided to strike out for Malawi, my destination in 1996 before lack of funds forced me to Zambia. I did not know if things would be better in Malawi, but I had to try.

Getting out of Mtabila wasn't so easy. Traveling legally in Tanzania was hard, and most refugees did not do it. To be legal, the refugee had to acquire a gate pass, which was not given to everyone. Tanzanian police would intimidate and imprison refugees found outside the camp without a gate pass. Because of this, I decided to pretend to be a Tanzanian citizen as I traveled.

Learn what made this camp dangerous for Burundians who lived there. Read "Unrest in Mtabila" on page 183.

I left Mtabila with a map of the journey sent to me by Emile. Immediately I changed my accent to Tanzanian Swahili, which I had learned from the locals working at the refugee camp as well as from listening to the radio. At the nearby Tanzanian city of Kigoma, I nervously boarded a train without a ticket. Taking advantage of the corruption common to the railroads, I negotiated my passage with the maintenance crew so that I could travel by train for almost two days. Next, I used my meager cash to buy bus tickets that took me close to the border with Malawi. The entire journey by train and bus covered almost 1500 kilometers (over 900 miles).

Arriving near the border on a Sunday morning, I realized I did not have enough money to keep traveling, and I was uncertain how to cross the border, so I looked for a church where I could attend services and ask for help.

MY DECEPTION

The first church I found was an Anglican church. As I knocked at the priest's door, I wondered what kind of a reception I would get since I had never been in an Anglican church before. As I waited for the priest, who was busy preaching at the first morning service, I contrived a plan. I might get a better reception, I reasoned, if I sang a solo in the church. I passed a note to the priest stating that I was a visitor wanting to sing.

Granted the opportunity, I explained to the congregation that I was a Tanzanian traveling to Malawi. I told them that I felt compelled to attend the service at this specific church instead of traveling on a Sunday. Then, accompanying myself on the church's keyboard, I began singing a song in Swahili that I had written after passing my high school exams. The chorus went like this, "Sing and praise the Lord Jesus; give Him praise because He saved you."

To my amazement, the entire congregation stood and joined in worship, singing and dancing to the music. I made many mistakes on the keyboard, but no one seemed to notice.

At the end of the service, people flocked to me. The priest, who had just learned that I was his guest, proudly introduced me to the rest of the congregation. Members of the choir approached me, asking if I would stay for a few days and teach them to sing and play the keyboard. I declined, stating that I had a previous commitment.

The priest invited me to his house for a meal and a night's lodging. He had told the congregation, after I finished my song, that God had arranged my singing at the Sunday morning service to encourage members of the church choir who felt insecure about their ability to sing. I explained to him that I had plans to visit a friend in Malawi but that I did not have enough money to take me there.

Though he gave me no money towards my transport, the priest did write a letter of introduction to the Anglican priest across the border. In that letter, he told of my financial

To better understand the practice of telling lies to survive, read "Refugee Deception" on page 185.

need. He wrote of my solo performance in church and highly recommended me as a singer with a passion for God. He concluded the letter by stating, "This young man is honest. Please consider helping him."

CROSSING THE BORDER

When I got to the Tanzanian-Malawian border, I went straight to the immigration office to ask for a border pass. I pretended to be a citizen of the Kyela District, on the Tanzanian side, sent by the Anglican priest to go preach in the Karonga District, on the Malawi side. Though shivering on the inside, I looked confident on the outside as I insisted the immigration officer issue the pass.

He did not. He told me I should go back to my district of origin and apply for one there. I argued that I was late for my preaching engagement and that people were getting tired of waiting, but he would not change his mind.

I left the immigration office disappointed that I did not get the border pass. If I reported to any district office they would have known I was lying and would have imprisoned me before sending me back to the refugee camp. On the other hand, I was relieved that, during the course of my conversation with the immigration official, he did not recognize that I was Burundian.

As I thought hard about what to do next, a bicycle-taxi asked if I wanted a ride across the border. I was doubtful it would work, but the operator convinced me he had helped many others to cross, so I climbed aboard.

We approached an area where people with no luggage went back and forth for local business exchange. If you were just crossing to make a purchase, you could usually get through. I wore all my clothes in layers, one on top of the other, and folded my luggage into a plastic shopping bag.

Without any problems, we passed through the border and onto Malawi soil. I immediately hailed another taxi which took me to the town of Karonga where Rev. Nyirenda (the Anglican priest) welcomed me like a son.

Rev. Nyirenda gave me enough money to cover my fare to Lilongwe, the capital of Malawi. I boarded a bus at around 7:00 p.m. and reached Lilongwe about 5:00 p.m. the following day. As I looked for a public phone to call Emile, I bumped into him—right there at the bus terminal. Emile and I spent a couple of days together in Lilongwe before he took me to Dzaleka Refugee Camp on July 27, 2003, to be registered as a refugee.

LIFE IN DZALEKA

Compared to the other camps I had lived in, Dzaleka offered some unique and desirable qualities. For one thing, refugees from Burundi,

Congo, Somalia, Rwanda, Ethiopia, and Sudan all lived together, without any demarcation or trouble. Furthermore, although the monthly rations allotted to the refugees did not cover all basic needs, they occasionally included a few luxury items like sugar, rice, and soap. Additionally, refugees had no problem getting passes to leave the camp, and no one mistreated refugees found outside the camp without a pass. Both the Malawi police and the local citizens acted peacefully toward the refugees.

However, Dzaleka had this in common with all other camps—a spirit of hopelessness. Many refugees had called Dzaleka home for years, but all their thoughts and dreams focused on getting out. Some dreamed of returning home but the conflicts which drove them into exile still raged. Others schemed to escape to supposedly better refugee camps, as I had just done. Resettlement ranked as the most popular option, but also the most difficult to attain. Those who did not get resettled or flee the camp eventually got involved in some income-generating activity to supplement their rations. But ALWAYS they dreamed of getting out.

Many Dzaleka refugees practiced *makanaki* – the possession of multiple ration cards.[1] One ration of food did not cover a person's need for the whole month. With few jobs available, refugees turned to cheating in order to get enough food for their families and earn a little extra for expenses like paraffin for lamps, clothes, shoes, a visit to the barber, and e-mail or phone time with friends and family abroad.

Because of my Christian values, I decided not to get involved in

---

1   Makanaki borrowed its name from Cyrille Makanaky, a Cameroonian soccer player good at dribbling and maneuvering the ball.

makanaki. Instead, I volunteered much of my time at a refugee church, Dzaleka Baptist. I used the various languages I knew to teach children of different nationalities. I trained the church choir. I also preached and interpreted during the services. All of this I did out of my love for God, as well as a misguided attempt to seek God's favor and win resettlement.

HEALING FROM ULCERS

Surviving on a single food ration without extra income proved difficult, as evidenced by the number of refugees practicing makanaki. The monthly ration for one refugee consisted of the following: 13 kg. (28.6 lbs.) of maize flour or rice, 8 kg. (17.6 lbs.) of beans or peas, some cooking oil, a bar of soap, some sugar, and some salt. For almost six years, I had been suffering from stomach ulcers, so I could not eat the beans or peas.[2]

Amazingly, however, my food supplies never ran out before the next month's distribution. When neighbors came asking for flour or rice, I would always have some to give them. I have no way of explaining how this happened except that God miraculously multiplied my food.

One Sunday, I received a phone call from Emmanuel Ngabo, a fellow refugee who at the time lived outside the camp in Lilongwe. He informed me of an evangelist named Mr. Hakiza who had arrived from Lukore, a refugee camp in Ngara District, Tanzania. A Rwandan who escaped that nation's 1994 genocide, Mr. Hakiza became a Christian in the refugee camp. After coming to faith, he began traveling and preaching about the difference that knowing God had made in his life. Now, he had come to preach at Dzaleka, and he needed a place to stay. Having

---

2   Many refugees develop ulcers as a result of stress and a very poor diet.

described to my friend Ngabo the kind of person he wanted to stay with, Ngabo thought of me. I had no money to feed Mr. Hakiza good food, but I told Nagabo I would share what little I had.

After two days living with me, Mr. Hakiza noticed that I had not cooked beans. Knowing the Burundians' love for beans, he asked about this. I explained that I had developed ulcers while at Meheba refugee camp in Zambia. Then Mr. Hakiza said, "Innocent, you have dedicated your life to God. Here is my advice: believe in your heart that God can and will heal your ulcers, because he loves you. Cook the food that you haven't been eating, then take it in with full trust in God and in his healing—do not doubt."

The following morning, I cooked peas and sweet potatoes, which I had not eaten for a long time due to the ulcers. When I ate these foods, nothing happened to me. I continued to reintroduce to my diet those foods which had previously triggered my ulcers—foods like beans, sweet potato, and Coca-Cola. I have never suffered from ulcers again.

WHY NOT ME, LORD?

As I have stated, part of my reason for leaving Mtabila Refugee Camp and illegally traveling to Malawi was my search for greater opportunity. I had heard of people like Emile who, after moving to Dzaleka Refugee Camp, had received a scholarship and achieved resettlement in the West. Despite the odds against that happening, I held onto the purposes for my life that God had begun revealing to me at Nyarugusu. *"He will reveal the means by which these purposes will be carried out,"* I whispered, to console myself. *"He must!"*

In 2004, one year after my arrival in Dzaleka, a pastor and a young Italian woman arrived in Dzaleka Refugee Camp. The woman, Florisa De Leo, had volunteered for a one-year position with the Malawi Economic Justice Network. The pastor, an African-American named Henry Joseph, led Capital City Baptist Church in Lilongwe.

They visited Dzaleka at the urging of Florisa, whose host family had hired a Congolese refugee to help improve their children's French language skills. This refugee told her about the camp and the desperation of the people living there. She felt the local church should get to know the refugees, seek to understand them, and work with them towards a better future.

Pastor Joseph agreed and took the initiative to arrange this visit to Dzaleka. While they talked with the camp administrator, I stood outside in a small group of people waiting to see the visitors and tell them our stories in the hope they would help us out.

Florisa emerged first from the administrator's office. She appeared reserved and kept staring at the small crowd of people who, in turn, stared at her. We mistook her quietness for pride. Nobody knew, until much later, how deeply moved she was by the great injustice done to thousands in this camp whose lives had been uprooted as a result of conflict.

That night, Florisa penned the following poem, titled "Russian Roulette."

This life is random – Rather than a lottery it is a Russian Roulette.

As I walk through the thousands upon thousands of souls

Parked in this refugee camp

I want to hide

Because pain gets in the way of thinking

How can we inflict death into the lives of one another?

It is grey, it is cold, and desperation screams at the top of its lungs

From the silent eyes of those observing me

While I watch them from the protection of my shell,

Various categories in this human zoo.

Isaiah 32:17 "Justice will produce lasting peace and security."

It was spoken longer ago than I can even count

And yet we have not learnt its lesson.

I put myself on the front line

And ask to see everyday

The grain of justice I can bring into a world so needy

Before I leave the burden of this responsibility

Into the hands of those who will just wash them clean

And decline the honour

Of serving the Prince of Peace.

When Pastor Joseph came out of the office, I rushed to greet him and introduced myself as a member of Dzaleka Baptist Church. He appeared delighted to talk with me, but the daylight had faded and the visitors had to leave. In parting, Pastor Joseph asked, "What do you want to do in life?" I told him, "I've dreamed of studying at university and of recording some of my songs." Right in front of the camp administrator's office, he prayed with me and gave me his phone number so we could keep in touch.

One week later, I traveled to Lilongwe and visited Pastor Joseph in his office at Capital City Baptist Church. He allowed me to use a church computer to send e-mails, and he promised to introduce me to a missionary and musician from Mississippi who would soon arrive in Malawi. Then I waited—again.

*   *   *

For an entire year after arriving in Dzaleka Refugee Camp, I had witnessed the resettlement of fellow refugees, some getting scholarships to study abroad. But I had not been successful in any of my applications. As a dedicated Christian, I asked God why He did not favor me instead of others with questionable morals. From time to time, I met tourists and short-term missionaries as they visited the camp. When I told them my story, they appeared to be moved and vowed to keep in touch or to try to help. After they left, however, I never heard from them again. I found this quite frustrating because I had always considered Westerners to be basically honest. Yet, these people constantly raised my hopes in vain.

Resenting what I perceived to be their thoughtless (if not outright malicious) treatment, I made a conscious decision not to trust anyone who promised help.

Against this backdrop, I met Pastor Henry Joseph.

CHAPTER 8

Leaving Dzaleka

Four months after our encounter in the refugee camp, Pastor Henry Joseph and his wife Debra introduced me to Chris and Connie Taylor who had arrived from Jackson, Mississippi. Chris worked as the church administrator at Capital City Baptist in Lilongwe, while he and Connie explored ways of implementing their vision for a music and dance school in Malawi.

When I met Chris, he asked to hear my story. Before I could finish, he began to weep. Composing himself, he asked what sort of help I wanted, and I repeated what I had told Pastor Joseph. "I would like to record my music or obtain a university scholarship." Our meeting ended without any formal promise, but Chris asked me to keep in touch with him.

Staying in touch with Chris proved to be a challenge. Perhaps God meant to teach me patience in the process. Sometimes Chris would ask me to meet him in Lilongwe, and I would spend hours waiting at the church office while he finished his work. On more than one occasion, I returned to the camp without meeting Chris. He knew I lived at the refugee camp without any source of income, so I expected Chris to reimburse my transportation costs. That didn't always happen, and I did not ask unless he offered it.

Because of this and memories of unfulfilled promises by other foreigners, I began to doubt that Chris would actually help. After three months of making a sustained effort to keep in touch, I quit trying.

When I finally borrowed a phone and called him again, over two months later, Chris expressed surprise and got very emotional. He said he had been looking for me during that time, but I did not have a personal phone, so he did not know how to reach me. At the end of this call, Chris asked me to meet him in Lilongwe.

"The time has arrived for you to come out of the refugee camp," said Chris, when we sat face to face again. The idea appealed to me, but I found it hard to believe, so I said nothing. He repeated these words again, thinking I had not understood.

"I heard you the first time," I said, "but I wondered whether you were serious."

"I'm not joking!" Chris stated emphatically. To prove it, he gave me money to go back to the camp and collect all my belongings. On April 8, 2005, I left Dzaleka Refugee Camp.

BUILDING INTIMACY

When I arrived back in Lilongwe, Chris took me to the Malawi Assemblies of God University. He had arranged for me to stay in a campus guestroom. The Taylors would pay for my accommodation and food on campus while they arranged a maintenance job for me at Capital City Baptist Church. As I waited to see how the Taylors would help me achieve either of my two objectives, I spent my days at the church sweeping the grounds, learning to clean the bathrooms and use the lawnmower, and washing cars.

While grateful for the opportunity being given me, I found it hard to fully trust Chris and Connie, having experienced the painful disappointment of unfulfilled promises from others. The Taylors tried to reassure me of their commitment, but I needed to see their promises lived out every day. Even then, I hesitated to put my confidence in them or anyone else.

For instance, I did not dare to ask when I lacked basics like soap or toothpaste, because I felt the Taylors would be irritated by my requests and stop supporting me. So, I prayed that God would move them to give me the things I needed—without asking. Initially it worked, but in the long-run it didn't. This forced me to trust them enough to ask.

Other experiences strengthened my faith as well. I had to stay on in the campus guestroom longer than expected. I did not know when I would move out, but every day I kept volunteering as a cleaner at Capital City Baptist Church. That summer, the Taylors returned to Mississippi for two months. I thought they would ask me to live in their house while they were gone, but they asked someone else. Nevertheless, they appointed people to look after me and cover my expenses in their absence.

A few days after the Taylors' departure, Pastor Henry Joseph approached and asked me to watch over his house while his family traveled to the U.S.A. "The reason I thought of you," he said, "Is that I trust you more than the church employees who normally guard the house."

That confused me. I wondered why, if he trusted me, he would not allow me to look after the house while living in it. Instead, he wanted to lock the house and have me watch from the outside, as any of the other guards would have done. In my culture, guarding someone's house or land is the most humble job an illiterate man can do to survive. I thought I had left the refugee camp because someone was willing to help me embrace my destiny—not to become the least in society.

For this and other unspoken reasons, I initially declined Pastor Joseph's offer to be his watchman. He expressed disappointment at my decision; so not wanting to offend the pastor, I asked for some time to think about his offer. I really wanted some time to cry about it, because I didn't want to do it. I could not help but compare myself to those who left the refugee camp before me. Some had obtained scholarships and were studying. Others had landed jobs. All could support their families one way or another. God surely wouldn't plan for me to be a watchman—would he?

After a few days of thinking and crying, I decided to accept the challenge to please my pastor. I also took the job because it would have been a greater shame to return to Dzaleka Refugee Camp than to guard my pastor's house.

When I told Pastor Joseph that I would accept his offer of employment, he expressed delight and promised to pay me part of my wages in advance. Little did he know what had been going on in my mind and in my heart.

LEARNING HUMILITY

My job involved guarding the pastor's house three days and three nights each week, buying food for their dog and feeding her, supervising the gardener, and e-mailing the pastor with updates on the house. I worked alongside the church guards in order to ensure security as well as to learn their job.

One particular watchman had guarded Capital City Baptist Church for seven years. He served as my instructor, telling me what time of night was safe for the guard to sleep and what time thieves would be most likely to strike. It amazed me that he sometimes slept under a tree from 11:00 p.m. to 5:00 a.m. One night, while he slept, the branch of a papaya fell near him. He woke thinking he heard bandits approaching and shouted *Akuba! Akuba!* meaning "Thieves! Thieves!" I laughed uncontrollably.

During my two months as a watchman, I never slept on a single shift. Every time I was tempted to put my head on my knees as I sat in my chair, I recalled Pastor Joseph's voice saying, "Innocent, I trust you. Please look after my house." When that happened, I got up and walked around the house until the urge to sleep left me.

When Pastor Joseph returned from his holiday, I expected him to give me some amazing gift from America—like a computer, a CD player, or clothes. To my surprise, all he gave me was the balance of my salary. In spite of this, our relationship deepened, and he showed me love and concern of incalculable worth.

> *Each person's journey is different from another's. We should deal with the challenges that come our way without comparing ourselves to others.*

I learned some important lessons from this experience. First, I came to recognize that each person's journey is different from another, so we should deal with the challenges that come our way without comparing ourselves to others. I also learned that we should not allow our dreams to become an obstacle to us embracing humble beginnings and seemingly slow progress.

Through this experience, I imagined what pain my father must have felt when, after having accomplished great financial success, the war forced him to work under people of lower social status than his employees in the old days. The day shifts as a watchman also gave me time to read my Bible and practice writing English.

Having gained my pastor's trust with a small job, he now trusted me with greater things.

ADAPTING TO A NEW CULTURE

Besides enduring bitterly cold June and July evenings as a watchman, I faced another challenge in the absence of Pastor Joseph and the Taylors. Nobody paid for my accommodation and food at the campus. The campus administration locked my room with all my possessions in it, and would not allow me to get in (or to get anything out) until they received payment. Again, my insecurity about people keeping their promises resurfaced. I did not know where to sleep or who to ask for help.

As I nursed my pain and worries on day-duty at the pastor's house, I received a call from Keta—a friend I met through Chris Taylor. She heard of my predicament and offered to either pay the campus bill or to take me to her house until the Taylors came back. In the end, Keta paid the bill.

When the Taylors returned to Malawi, they invited me to live with them. Living with an American family gave me an interesting glimpse into a totally different culture. Growing up in Congo, I assumed all children would display total and unconditional obedience to their parents or to anyone older. So it shocked me to see parents treating their children as peers, giving them the option of declining a request for help, for example.

Our differences in communication resulted in many misunderstandings. In my culture, not hurting someone with the truth was the priority. This stood in stark contrast to the Taylor family's open expression of their opinions. As a new family member, I tried to keep good rapport with everyone, so I found it difficult to express myself as freely as they expected.

Aside from these challenges, living with the Taylors and witnessing their interactions as a family really expanded my horizons. I realized all that I had missed as a child, both because of growing up in tough conditions and because of the African culture. When I observed their children choosing not to eat certain foods and opting for something else (and their parents accommodating them) I thought of how I had to eat whatever was put on my plate, without complaining. Hunger was the only other option. And when the Taylors expressed concern about every little illness of their children, it reminded me of many wounds I never mentioned to my brothers, let alone my dad, since they were not life threatening. Perhaps I also feared the pain of some traditional remedies my family would apply.

OFFERED A SCHOLARSHIP

Ten months after I left Dzaleka Refugee Camp, the Taylors informed me that they had found a scholarship for me. I could apply to the school of my choice, and the scholarship would pay for my education at that school. The news thrilled me beyond description. The biggest of all my dreams would soon become reality.

Immediately I began contacting Francophone (French-speaking) universities in the African countries of Burkina Faso, D.R. Congo, and Senegal, and also in Quebec, Canada, with the goal of becoming a lawyer who could administer justice in Burundi. Elation gave way to severe disappointment as none of these schools responded.

After writing to all the schools I could think of, Chris suggested that I apply at the Malawi Assemblies of God University—the campus where I lived after leaving Dzaleka.

"That is a bizarre idea," I thought at first. I had never had any desire to go to Bible school, in part because I had seen Bible school graduates returning to their local churches with big heads, wanting to lord it over those with no formal training. Also, despite being a committed Christian, I believed that a Bible school certificate did not offer what my country and my people needed to end their suffering. I reasoned that they needed people with law degrees who would understand and be able to do the right thing.

Finally, instructors at the Malawi Assemblies of God University conducted classes in English. Throughout my life, I had studied in French. I could not understand and write English well enough to function at the college level—or so I told myself.

For several weeks, I rejected the idea of applying to the Bible school. But after I had exhausted all of my previous attempts at gaining entrance to post-secondary schools, I decided to give this bizarre idea a try. I applied to the Assemblies of God University in Lilongwe, Malawi. To my surprise, I received a positive response from the school's registrar general.

My acceptance gave everyone a reason for celebration—everyone but me. Not wanting to offend anyone, I painted a smile on my face, but my heart did not rejoice. I had absolutely no desire to attend Bible school.

BIRTH OF THERE IS HOPE

My first semester at the Assemblies of God University began in February of 2006. At that time, I still couldn't get excited about the only university that had accepted me. "If my dad were still alive," I consoled myself, "at least he would be happy." Dad cared so much for the Bible.

From the day I received the registrar's positive response until the first day of classes, I kept praying that God would reveal why I had to attend Bible school. I resolved not to pray another prayer until I got an answer to this one.

Eighteen days after the semester began, on February 27, I received my answer. As I sat in a preaching class, God put a clear and very strong conviction in my heart. I understood, for the first time, that I had been placed at this school to acquire the tools I needed to help people living in refugee camps. God was preparing me, a refugee since birth, to return to my fellow refugees with a message of hope.

My heart groaned as I thought of the pain and misery endured by refugees. Deep within me, I knew that I should take responsibility to provide these displaced people with things that would give them confidence and a future—like access to higher education and technology, an outlet for their creativity, the Bible, and so much more.

Tears formed in the corners of my eyes as I realized the immensity of this assignment. Still an asylum seeker myself, I could not conceive of doing this on my own. How could I, a man without dignity and still needing hope, give hope to others? How could I be trusted to accomplish so much in a foreign country when I did not even have the right to work here?

I left class to wash the tears from my face and returned, relieved that no one had noticed. *"I am willing to do what you have put in my heart,"* I told God, *"but I need to know where and how to begin."*

The conviction given me that day in early 2006 became almost an obsession. I thought about it day and night. I dared to share it with a few close friends who encouraged me to pursue the calling but offered few ideas of how to begin. Only Rhonda Allen, an American missionary teacher at the university, gave me practical insight that helped me get started.

Rhonda taught my Principles of Teaching class. Her instruction impressed me, and I reasoned that, as a Western missionary, she had had experience in raising and managing funds. So I scheduled a meeting and told her my life's story. I finished by explaining to Rhonda the vision

God had put on my heart and my confusion as to where to begin. She encouraged me to spend more time pondering the vision and drawing out more details, and to take one step at a time, instead of trying to accomplish everything at once.

To demonstrate her confidence in my calling, Rhonda purchased twenty-three Bibles in Kinyarwanda[1] to distribute at Dzaleka Refugee Camp and made herself available for more counseling going forward.

I followed Rhonda's advice, writing down every thought that came to mind about the work I imagined doing with refugees. I named the organization "Hope to the Hopeless" and set its objectives as sponsoring post-secondary education, fostering the arts, and supporting the work of churches.

Not until I met an American couple named LeRoy and Cindy Metzger, however, did the organization actually begin to take shape.

I met the Metzgers at a prayer night organized by Chris and Connie Taylor at My Brother's Keeper School of Music and Movement, which they had successfully launched in Lilongwe. I soon learned that the Metzgers had been leading Hope Chapel in Hawaii when God called them to Africa, Malawi in particular.

When I saw them again at Capital City Baptist Church, the Metzgers mentioned their plans to visit friends at the refugee camp, and they invited me to go with them. On the way to the camp, Cindy asked me to tell my story. So I explained about being born in a refugee camp and how both parents had died. Then I told her about my vision for Hope to the Hopeless.

---

1   Kinyarwanda—The official language of Rwanda, spoken by many Dzaleka residents.

Before visiting Dzaleka with the Metzgers, I had applied as a refugee to the camp administration for recognition of the new organization. I had been granted a piece of land in the camp on the condition that something would be established there within two months. If not, the land would be used for other purposes.

The Metzgers expressed interest in my story and vision. When we arrived at the camp, we went to the ground I had been given and prayed for God's will to be done.

The following morning, Cindy called. "Innocent," she said, "last night Leroy and I prayed about your vision. God confirmed that we need to stand by your side in whatever way we can. We don't have money, but we have friends. Put your story in writing, and we will send it to our friends, asking for donations."

A few days later, LeRoy, Cindy and I, along with four other people, formed a Hope to the Hopeless steering committee. The Metzgers hosted the first meeting of this committee in their home.

During the second meeting, LeRoy and Cindy challenged the other steering committee members to start preparing the ground and hiring people to dig the foundations for a planned recreation center on the land that had been given to us. Committee members spent a long time debating the idea of starting with no assurance that any money would come in, but in the end we decided to trust God. We opened a corporate account at a local bank and sent out a newsletter explaining our purpose and asking for donations. We also selected some refugees to start digging the foundations.

Three days later, as I attended classes at the university, I received a phone call from the foreman asking for sand, cement, quarry-stone, and other materials, because they had almost finished digging the foundations. I asked him to wait until the end of class, and I started wondering what to do since we had no money that I knew of in our bank account.

I called LeRoy to find out if he had received any feedback from the newsletter. He had not yet received a single e-mail or phone call. I checked my e-mails to see if anyone had written and found one single message from Phil and Barbara Buckman, Welsh friends of the Metzgers. They read the newsletter and wanted to encourage me to continue obeying God, but they made no mention of money. Finally, I checked the balance in our bank account.

To my great surprise, I learned it contained over US$2,000. I could not believe it. I thought the clerk had made a mistake, so I asked another clerk to verify the balance. That clerk gave me exactly the same figure.

I found it incredible that we could receive all this money without anyone mentioning it. On the following day, LeRoy and Chenela, a friend from Capital City Baptist Church and a member of our steering committee, bought and delivered the building supplies for the foundation of the recreation center. Hope to the Hopeless sprang to reality.

To the Reader: In the chapters that follow, my story and the story of Hope to the Hopeless (later renamed There is Hope) will entwine. Who I am and what has happened to me since leaving Dzaleka Refugee Camp is inseparable from this organization which offers a future to so many displaced people. We are one and the same.

CHAPTER 9

No Longer a Refugee

Work began on the recreation center in July 2006. One month later, as workers completed the building's foundation, the funds which had miraculously appeared in our checking account ran out.

Earlier, I had approached the camp administrator with my vision of what Hope to the Hopeless could bring to the residents of Dzaleka. I saw the recreation center as a place where refugees could engage in on-line education as well as access communication tools that would link them to the outside world.[1] People could also visit the center to get away from the dreariness of life, to check news, and to watch videos that would both inspire and entertain.

---

[1]   In 2006, if refugees wanted to check e-mail, they had to ask for camp exit passes, pay for transportation to the Malawi's capital city, and pay to use computers at Internet cafés.

The camp administrator had expressed surprise and excitement at the idea of a recreation center. At that time, Dzaleka had no such facility. "Bring me a drawing of what you want to build," said the official, indicating he would base his decision on that illustration.

An acquaintance at Capital City Baptist Church worked at a drafting company. "Give me a simple sketch of the rooms," she said, "and I'll take care of everything." In a few weeks, the woman handed me a professionally done drawing at no charge. When I had shown the drawing to the camp administrator and the person in charge of camp construction, they could not believe the quality of the plans. They gave Hope to the Hopeless the best site on which to build this beautiful building—and all this with zero budget.

Now, the dormancy of this construction project disappointed me, and I waited impatiently for the fulfillment of the dream. Meanwhile, I visited the camp frequently to gather information on the needs of the refugees and on what could improve their lives. I also spent time writing strategies and broadening the dream.

Unfortunately, no additional money appeared in our bank account, so the camp administrator took back the land and everything contributed to the construction of the center died in its foundations.

Red Cross Malawi built a recreational center soon after the Hope to the Hopeless project expired, and eventually Jesuit Refugee Services built an on-line learning center at Dzaleka. Though it frustrated me that we had not been able to follow through on our first project, it pleased me that the refugees got what they needed.

Years later, I consider our abandoned foundation like seeds buried in the ground. They took time to germinate, but when they finally burst forth, they did so with great force and today are visible to all. If the funds necessary to build the recreation center had come quickly, I would have missed a lot of reflection, learning, and planning time that eventually contributed to the success of our organization.

Still, I felt pain at the sight of the arrested building project. Refugees asked me what happened, and many saw the lack of activity on the construction site as a failure. They had seen my *wazungu* (white people) on site and wondered if I had lost credibility with them or had chosen the wrong people.[2] Some even wondered if I had misappropriated the money the *wazungu* had given me, although truthfully I never found out whether that first US$2,000 came from Africa or elsewhere.

Surely the international NGOs working at Dzaleka assumed that Hope to the Hopeless would be another initiative that would only last until it met the first obstacle, which is typical of so many refugee initiatives. They fail either because of corruption or lack of planning.

But the demise of the center did produce some positive results. For one thing, I faced lots of questions for which I had no answers that could be easily understood. This helped me to build the skills I needed to answer the public's inquiries in simple terms—diplomatically.

For another, the refugees had seen me bring a big vision into the camp, and because of this many opened up and talked to me about their needs and their plans. They shared their own dreams with me because they saw that I could think outside the box.

I also began drafting a constitution for Hope to the Hopeless

---

2   When many rural Africans see *wazungu* involved with a project, they expect whatever is being done to be accomplished in a matter of days—so strong is their attitude that white people make the world go round.

and inviting reputable people to serve on the organization's board of trustees—both of which we needed to register with the government of Malawi.

ANOTHER PAIR OF HANDS

In September of 2006, Florisa De Leo, who I had met two years before at Dzaleka Refugee Camp, e-mailed Pastor Henry Joseph. "Has the church begun to work with the refugees?" she asked, adding, "I believe God wants me to go back to Dzaleka."

During her previous stay in Malawi, Florisa had told Pastor Joseph about seeing in her mind's eye a wooden cross like that of Jesus' being carried by the hands of one person, although that person was not Jesus.

"The message I felt God wanted to convey to me was this: if more people came under the cross to support it, its weight would be manageable," she said later. That's when she convinced Pastor Joseph to visit Dzaleka and when they met me for the first time, but she had no idea of what had transpired since our 2004 meeting.

Pastor Henry replied to Florisa's e-mail advising her to travel to Malawi to meet with me and share ideas.

A short time later, I sat in Pastor Joseph's office at Capital City Baptist Church. "Do you have a girlfriend?" asked Henry Joseph. When I replied that I didn't, he said "Would you marry my daughter?"

"Would you trust me to marry your daughter?" I responded, and we both laughed. Then Pastor Joseph told me that a young lady who he affectionately called his daughter wanted to come to Malawi to meet me and to explore the possibility of working together to help refugees.

"Who knows," he motioned, "maybe she will end up being your wife."

Florisa came to Malawi over the Christmas holidays of 2006. We spent two weeks talking about the camp, the needs of the people, and what we could do. We also spent considerable time talking about our backgrounds. I did not reveal all because I didn't really know her. When it was her turn, Florisa's openness impressed me, and her transparency stunned me. I felt unworthy to be told some very personal things.

During her brief stay, Florisa and I visited Dzaleka with my friend Joshua Chikamata to capture images for a video showing the needs of refugees in Malawi and promoting the vision of Hope to the Hopeless. We also worked together on the last draft of the organization's constitution. Both Florisa and the board of trustees thought the name of the organization should be changed. "To have a negative word like *hopeless* in the name paints a bad picture," she reasoned. Florisa suggested changing the name of the organization to There is Hope.

That suggestion resonated with all of us, and we wrote the new name into our constitution.

FREEDOM TO CROSS BORDERS

On January 7, 2007, Florisa returned to England. Arriving home, she kept in touch by e-mail, and she called me regularly to discuss new developments regarding There is Hope. Over time, our phone calls became more frequent, and the time spent talking about our personal lives grew considerably.

The next two years proved quiet and uneventful. I studied full-time and in my spare time gathered greater insight into the needs of the Dzaleka residents, while searching for the right solutions to their problems.

One thing continued to hamper my efforts to earn my degree and grow this fledgling organization—the world still looked at me as an asylum seeker. I often compare a refugee to a match. A match is expected to be in a matchbox. Anyone who discovers a match outside the matchbox will try to put it back in. In the same way, a refugee is expected to be in a refugee camp. Anyone who discovers a refugee outside the camp will try to put him back in. There is little freedom of movement.

My asylum-seeker status limited my activities to those of a student at

Get Florisa's take on the untapped potential inside the refugee matchbox. Read "A Match Set Alight" on page 189.

the Assemblies of God School of Theology. I had been invited to go on school trips to Zambia, Mozambique, Zimbabwe, and Botswana, but could not venture outside Malawi since I had no passport. Also, leading There is Hope turned out to be nearly impossible as a displaced person. I needed a work permit to do so, and there was no way for me to get one without a valid passport.

Burundi had experienced a change of government, and the army was now composed of Hutu as well as Tutsi soldiers. It was a stable period for the country, and I felt I could travel there without fear.

So in July 2007, I decided to take matters into my own hands. I asked everyone I knew to contribute to my travel back to Burundi. People gave generously, and I started off for Malawi's border with Tanzania.

Since I had no legal travel document, I once again put on my act.

From Lilongwe to the Malawi border, I acted as a Malawian planning to visit Tanzania. Because I had lived in Malawi for nearly five years, I had become fluent in Chichewa, the predominant Malawian language. But then after crossing the border into Tanzania, I acted as a Tanzanian, and when I neared Tanzania's border with Burundi, I acted as a Burundian— paying a small amount of money to cross, since I didn't have a passport.

Arriving in Burundi, I went straight to my family's home in the village of Gitaza and obtained an identity card from the local authorities. I had been born in Congo, which I was told would complicate the process, so the identity card stated that I had been born in Burundi. Next, I gathered the necessary documents to apply for a passport, and with a little help from a family friend in government, I received this precious document in a matter of days.

Words cannot describe the peace and confidence I experienced as I traveled back to Malawi. I felt like a *mzungu*—able to travel anywhere and do anything. Borders at which I had, in the past, changed my identity to escape detection I now passed through without fear, openly declaring who I was. Returning to Malawi, I used my newly acquired proof of Burundian citizenship to apply for a student visa. My passport also opened the opportunity for international travel. Within months, the Movement for African National Initiatives invited me to speak in South Africa about working with refugees, and I took my first airplane ride ever. At the age of twenty-seven, I was no longer a refugee.

For more on my newfound sense of freedom, read "Children Waving at Airplanes" on page 191.

On December 31, 2007, the government of Malawi formally issued a certificate of incorporation to There is Hope , and we had the official status we needed to move forward with our vision: *Seeing refugees, asylum seekers, and vulnerable people in the host community rise above difficult circumstances by fully utilizing their potential, being self-sufficient, and making a positive contribution to society.*

OUR ROMANCE BLOSSOMS

Meanwhile, Florisa had continued, since her December 2006 visit, to pursue the idea of joining There is Hope. She took several measures to confirm the wisdom of the big life change, including regularly meeting with the leaders of her home church for accountability and training in Uganda and Central African Republic for work in Africa. In July 2008, a year and a half after I had last seen her, Florisa came to Malawi for a month, bringing senior leaders of International Teams, a Christian organization which works with various underprivileged groups. Florisa had applied to join There is Hope under their supervision.

Besides our mutual interest in refugee work, a romantic relationship had blossomed as we talked on the phone and communicated by e-mail. Early in 2008, we'd speak every few days about There is Hope and about personal matters. Florisa had shared with the International Teams leaders that we had feelings for each other, and it was during this trip that a partnership between There is Hope and International Teams began. There is Hope would benefit from this relationship in terms of accountability, training, and recruitment of more volunteers through their network. International Teams would benefit in extending their work to refugees in Malawi.

Besides observing this milestone for There is Hope, Florisa and I began dating with the full consent and counsel of her sponsoring organization, and with Pastor Henry Joseph as our accountability partner.

Early in November 2008, Florisa moved to Malawi after raising enough financial support to cover her living expenses as a volunteer. This crucial time put all of our good intentions to the test. I enjoyed working with Florisa. This frequently took place using her laptop and whatever Internet connection we could find—mainly the one at Capital City Baptist Church. I directed the activities of There is Hope, and she coordinated the work. The needs of the refugees sometimes overwhelmed us, and it frustrated us that we had so little to help them with in those early days.

Florisa and I had been invited to attend a conference organized by International Teams in Nairobi, Kenya in March 2009. As we took off from Lilongwe International Airport, my heart swelled with exhilaration at the incredible path my life had taken – from a childhood spent running after the occasional car appearing in our Congolese village (usually driven by white American missionaries) to today as I traveled in a plane with my white girlfriend.

During the flight, Florisa wore a thumb ring. She jokingly moved it to her ring finger and glancing at me as if to say, "Next time we fly we'll be husband and wife." The cabin attendants served lunch, and Florisa laughed as I put a packet of unused sugar in my trouser pocket. She gently assured me that we would not be short of sugar at the conference, but old habits die hard.

I asked Florisa if she was happy with our relationship and if she had any doubts about me. "I am happy," she replied.

With that, I reached into my trouser pocket for what Florisa thought was the sugar packet. Instead, out came a ring box. I proceeded to drop the box on the floor of the plane as I tried to open it, perhaps due to my shaking hands. Retrieving the box, I succeeded in opening and holding it in front of her, while speaking the four little words I had rehearsed. "Will you marry me?" I asked. "Yes," said Florisa.

On August 15, 2009, Pastor Henry Joseph presided over our wedding ceremony at Capital City Baptist Church

For insight to the challenges of our multi-cultural marriage, read "Our Afro-European Merger" on page 193.

in Lilongwe, Malawi. Both of Florisa's parents, her brother, and her aunt traveled to Africa for the first time to watch us exchange vows. I had the joy of hosting my brother Hari who traveled to our wedding from his home in Tanzania's Kigoma region. My cousin Vincent also attended, representing our clan in my home country of Burundi, and Vincent's sister Mwavita came to our wedding from Mozambique's Maratane Refugee Camp.

Over 400 people from several continents and life-styles came to the wedding party to cheer and support us. Hundreds more from North America, Africa, Europe, and Australia sent gifts and cards to help us celebrate.

Our wedding brought me great joy, but also on that day I missed Dad and Mum more than ever. I wished they had lived to see Florisa and me united in marriage. I longed to feel the touch of their hands and to hear their words bless our new family.

CHAPTER 10

The Growth of Hope

What I have seen, since that day in 2006 when God called me to work with refugees, is a dream translated into reality. I have watched people who knew nothing about There is Hope completely embrace this organization as their own, and I've seen the shedding of tears as the lives of countless displaced men, women, and children have been transformed.

When the idea for There is Hope first occurred to me, one of my next thoughts was, "Who will join something started by a man with no status and no money?"

Indeed, who could have imagined that an organization which today offers university scholarships, early childhood education, seed money for small businesses, training to acquire a skill and generate income, food for prisoners, and artificial limbs for the disabled, would be established and directed by a refugee?

Well, that is exactly what has happened, but not overnight.

I like to quote Thomas Edison, who invented the light bulb after 999 failed attempts. "Our greatest weakness lies in giving up," said Edison. "The most certain way to succeed is to try just one more time."

It is often said that provision follows vision, but in my experience that path is not always quick or straight forward. What do we do when God gives us a vision and we believe the timing is right, but provision delays? This is the story of There is Hope. This is my story.

*   *   *

After spending the initial sum of US$2,000 in 2006 to construct foundations for a community center inside Dzaleka Refugee Camp, There is Hope operated for three-and-one-half years with almost no budget.

During that time, I finished my studies at the Malawi Assemblies of God University and received my diploma.

Also while waiting for God's provision, I continued to visit Dzaleka camp, forming relationships, assessing the needs of residents, and devising strategies. As I mentioned earlier, a group of people dedicated to helping the vulnerable agreed to serve as the organization's board of trustees, and in December 31, 2007, the government of Malawi officially recognized There is Hope.

But it was not until Florisa with International Teams joined our organization in November 2008 that There is Hope began to attract a variety of partners in the United Kingdom, Italy, and the United States. Their financial support made it possible to implement our vision.

Early in 2009, There is Hope launched its first major initiative by awarding a single university scholarship.

You see, the best durable solution the international community can offer a refugee is repatriation—the opportunity to go back home. And the best way to assure successful repatriation and prevent future conflicts is education.

Resettlement to another country is a solution desired by many refugees, but it's not the best solution. When you are resettled, you are pulled up by the roots from the culture you know, and you face the challenges of learning a new language and finding a job in a country that may not recognize your qualifications. We've even heard of doctors cleaning toilets.

Then there's the matter of adapting to the weather, since most refugees resettle in colder climates. Finally, resettlement adds to the braindrain, siphoning men and women who could contribute to society in their homelands.

Yes, repatriation is better, but lack of opportunity often stands in the way of repatriation because there is nothing to go home to. Before fleeing their countries, many refugees cultivated the earth. When they fled, that land was almost always taken from them or at least occupied by others. Returning home to fight the occupiers can create conflict and cost lives. Many refugees either can't go home or turn down offers of voluntary repatriation because they have nothing to return to.

But if, while exiled to a refugee camp like Dzaleka, refugees attend university in preparation for a career that does not depend on the land, they may be able to return home and successfully provide for themselves. Even if they decide not to go back, they have a greater chance of being accepted elsewhere if they possess a degree or a skill.

For this very reason, There is Hope facilitates and awards refugee scholarships. We do so not just to meet the individual's needs but with the idea that education transforms the lives of the refugee's family and all those around them, wherever they go. It is the best way to assure successful repatriation and prevent future conflicts.

Africa is rife with examples of both men and women leaders who have returned to their countries of origin after living as refugees. Many of these earned university level degrees while in exile. Most of today's South African leaders received their education as refugees outside their birth country. The current presidents of the Democratic Republic of Congo, Rwanda, and Burundi lived as refugees at one time, receiving their education outside their countries.

By making it possible for refugees to seek education beyond secondary school, There is Hope believes it is helping to prepare future leaders who will return to their countries and contribute towards a durable peace where people will not be forced to leave their homes.

As its first major initiative, There is Hope helped Rwandan refugee Zaituna Ubabona in January 2009 to access a scholarship and begin studies for a three-year nursing diploma. Since that time, through its Refugee University Scholarship Program, There is Hope has assisted numerous men and women to study in fields ranging from medicine and IT to business management and community development. These scholarship recipients would otherwise have been unable to afford a university education.

While some refugees can improve their prospects by studying at a university, others simply need a hand up to develop a profession or skill they already possess. Many people living at Dzaleka Refugee Camp have the skills required to be financially independent, but they need starting capital and a little encouragement.

Working with a refugee church, There is Hope began a microloan program in 2009 by advancing 20,000 Malawian Kwacha (about US$80) to two refugee women with the skills to make traditional Burundian cassava bread (*ubuswage*) and sell it in Dzaleka's market.

To understand the vital role faith plays in the life of a refugee, turn to page 197.

As a condition of the loan, we required the first two women to name four more women to receive the principle when it was repaid and to coach those women in their start-up businesses. From these humble beginnings, our microloan program has grown and helped hundreds of refugees earn what they need to supply their basic needs.

In recent years, There is Hope has explored and adopted many other ways of walking alongside refugees and asylum seekers residing in Dzaleka Refugee Camp. To read about the organization's amazing growth, visit *www.thereishopemalawi.org*.

PERSONAL AND CORPORATE TRIALS

I must honestly tell you that this growth has not occurred along a direct and ascending trajectory. As stated earlier, God's vision has not always been followed immediately by his provision, as evidenced by our three-and-a-half-year financial drought. Nor have all of our initiatives proved immediately successful. But like Edison, we've operated on the principle that "the most certain way to succeed is to try just one more time."

I personally, and the organization corporately, have both endured trials in recent years that tested the veracity of my faith and my original vision for There is Hope.

My Personal Trial–On August 13, 2010, almost one year after I married Florisa at Capital City Baptist Church in Lilongwe, my wife gave birth to our first child, a daughter we named Mwiza Aurora.

Mwiza was born with a severe brain malformation. Despite our best efforts to seek medical and divine healing for our dear daughter, Mwiza died before reaching the age of two. The experience left Flo and me physically, emotionally, and spiritually exhausted.

The Organizational Trial – Although we never have, and never will, pretend responsibility for the short-term survival needs of the refugees, There is Hope appealed to its international partners early in 2012 for funds to help with a severe food shortage at Dzaleka. We

For a deeper understanding of this personal trial, read "Mwiza: The Big Impact of a Brief Life" on page 201.

did so in response to a request for help made during a meeting to which we had been explicitly invited. The World Food Program hosted this meeting.

In our brief history, we had never witnessed such generosity from the outside as that which appeared in response to our appeal. However, the visibility of There is Hope's contribution to Dzaleka's welfare triggered some underlying insecurities and animosity. At least one person working at UNHCR Malawi and its local partners circulated false accusations against There is Hope to his superiors. This resulted in the rejection of our food donation and the questioning of our legitimacy.

The false accusations, as reported by a Malawi government official in charge of refugees, included:

- That I am a refugee and not legally allowed to work in Malawi. *In fact, I have a passport and a work permit issued by the very same governmental department.*
- That I steal money raised under the pretense of helping refugees. *In fact, all There is Hope accounts are audited yearly by certified auditors and this government office has received all audit reports.*
- That There is Hope only helps Burundian refugees. *In fact, the statistics in our annual report, which this government office also receives, prove otherwise.*

The situation that unfolded in the spring and summer of 2012 was utterly unbelievable. It was clear the attacks were deliberate and that our multiple attempts to discuss the matter were receiving no attention. Having done everything we knew how to do locally, we resorted to logging an official complaint with the headquarters of UNHCR in Geneva, Switzerland. It broke my heart that the food, stored in a warehouse just 45 kilometers (28 miles) from Dzaleka, could only be released with the intervention of someone halfway across the world, while educated, capable people given stewardship over their fellow Africans squabbled over territory.

After wrestling with this issue for six months, UNHCR in Geneva appointed Mr. George Kuchio as its Country Representative for Malawi. Mr. Kuchio had the mandate of looking into the matter. Within a few weeks of his arrival, the food aid (70 metric tons of maize and US$18,000 for the World Food Program to purchase additional food) reached Dzaleka's refugee population in December of 2012. Since then, an organization that was the major source of allegations against There is Hope has lost its contract to operate within Dzaleka Refugee Camp.

This incident took its toll on us, although it eventually built our faith and determination. I have since been grateful for the openness and professionalism of Mr. Kuchio and the ensuing positive relationship with UNHCR Malawi. Unfortunately, the world of relief and development is not free from power struggles.

*   *   *

As with many trials, however, the good resulting from these experiences outweighs the bad over time.

For one thing, our dear daughter's infirmity has opened our eyes to the plight of refugee parents with children similarly disabled. By the same token, seeing us wrestle with Mwiza's health problems broke a huge stigma that threatened to isolate people with disabled children.

Before Mwiza's birth, it was assumed that if you are a Christian, and especially if you are a pastor, as I am known, nothing bad will ever happen to you. Perceptions in the camp have radically changed for the better since I began sharing about our trials and Flo began speaking honestly with the women of the camp about her pain and her love for Mwiza.

As for the food crisis of 2012, we remain confident that other organizations working alongside There is Hope to assist residents of Dzaleka Refugee Camp have a better understanding of our motives. Together, we can be even more effective in offering hope.

FOUNDATIONS FINALLY RISE

In 2006, Hope for the Hopeless (later renamed There is Hope) roared to life and quickly retreated with a whimper. Within a month of beginning construction on a community center inside Dzaleka Refugee Camp, the project ground to a halt due to the lack of funding.

Having sustained this injury early in our existence, it is significant to note that eight and one-half years later, on February 12, 2014, There is Hope hosted a large crowd at the dedication of a newly constructed community center less than 200 meters from the front gates of Dzaleka Refugee Camp.

Attendees at this dedication included local chiefs and representatives of district government, leaders of various national groups within the camp, There is Hope staff members and trustees, and the team of workers who built the center. Covered by the local media, the ceremony featured speeches from many people, performances from refugee and Malawian artists, and the cutting of the ribbon to formally open the center.

Unlike our 2006 construction project *inside* the camp, which never rose above its foundations, this fine-looking community center stands today just *outside* the main camp entrance. Today, it is used by both refugees and residents of the villages surrounding the camp for weddings, conferences, and other community events.

A building adjacent to the center provides classroom space for vocational training courses open to both refugees and local populations. There is Hope also supports the effort of community based organizations to establish and sustain Early Childhood Development Centers in local villages.

Our recent emphasis on working with underserved communities around Dzaleka Refugee Camp stems from the desire for refugees to see themselves as having something to contribute to those around them, and for local people to view refugees as a blessing rather than a curse. By bringing them together, we expect both populations to better understand and lift each other up.

*   *   *

Was our 2006 vision for a community center simply premature, or did the provision arrive too late? I believe we cannot make provision a condition to our pursuit of God's vision. We need to push on, use what we have, and keep our eye on the desired outcome. We need to be willing to make sacrifices and not have our entire wish list checked off before moving forward. Sometimes we find provision along the way.

Above all, we need to be patient. I recently learned of a man from India named Dashrath Manjhi who, following the death of his wife for lack of immediate medical care, cut down a mountain single-handedly over a period of twenty-two years to create a shortcut of 1 kilometer instead of 70 kilometers between his village and the nearest hospital. This reminded me of how important it is to be persistent and take the long-term view of our work.

Anyone's efforts toward positive change in the world are significant, whether their effects are visible now or in the years to come.

CHAPTER 11

A Refugee for Life

My parents fled from their beloved Burundi seven years before my birth. For twenty-seven years, I lived as a refugee in five settlements and camps situated in four African countries. Now in my upper 30s, I continue serving refugees through There is Hope.

My plans and ambitions revolve around stopping the causes of displacement and positively impacting the lives of those who have been displaced. For this reason, I refer to myself as "a refugee for life." I no longer live as a refugee, but I cannot possibly detach myself from my past or from the people at the center of my concern.

The previous chapters have given you a glimpse of major stories in my life and the lives of refugees in general. I am humbled whenever I interact with refugees, to see their trust and openness in telling me their painful experiences. I can't help feeling that my painful past is nothing compared to what many have endured.

That said, I have learned some things from over three decades of experience with displacement. I will share them in this final chapter.

PAIN AS A FACT OF LIFE

Most African mothers believe that a normal child must cry at birth. If it does not, the mother will inflict a small amount of pain to make the baby cry. While I do not agree entirely with this concept, it does contain some truth.

A mother's womb provides for all of an embryo's needs, with little effort on the baby's part. When the baby is born, however, everything is new and unpleasant. Breathing on its own, feeling cold or hot, and later experiencing physical and emotional pain as a fact of life, the baby who will grow to adulthood starts to cry.

During my 27 years as a refugee and now as an advocate for refugees, I have learned that:

- Shared pain brings hope. When people go through a painful situation, they usually think it is the worst thing in the world and it is only happening to them. Opening up and sharing their pain with others, however, brings a realization that they are not alone. This results in hope and hope generates the needed energy, without ignoring the pain, to keep on with life.
- Pain has multiple causes. It can be self-inflicted, caused by others, or caused by nature. In a refugee situation, pain can be initiated by a handful of people, yet felt by millions of innocents.

- Our pain can benefit others. When we overcome pain, it is an occasion to help others, provided we do not ascribe our deliverance to ourselves.

When people hear my story and the stories of other overcomers, they often praise us as being resilient, inspirational, or otherwise special. It is hard for me to accept such praise, because when I was in the middle of my struggle, I was as miserable as anyone else. Likewise, when I came out of my situation, many people stretched out their hands to me and pulled or pushed me along. If any human beings deserve praise, these people do. I would not be where I am today without assistance from organizations such as UNHCR, as well as individuals who offered practical help at various stages of my journey. They share an equal part in my story.

To all who suffer in exile: take comfort in the hands reaching out to you.

EMERGENCY RESPONSE VERSUS RECOVERY WORK

Growing up in refugee settlements and camps, I always dreamed of becoming an influential leader. I was inspired primarily by the stories of Melchiore Ndadaye, the first popularly elected president of Burundi, and of South Africa's Nelson Mandela. I knew from a young age that higher education would make my dreams a realistic goal.

At the same time, I saw all around me crowds of vulnerable women with no education and few skills, struggling to survive when forced to live in a camp with no arable land or when their provider-husbands had died. I saw equally despondent fishermen, herded to camps in remote areas with no lakes or rivers nearby. These men watched their skills evaporate like puddles in the hot sun. They took a long time to adapt to their new circumstances and relied solely on emergency relief, which is insufficient to live an adequate life.

On the other hand, I witnessed a few displaced people who quickly adapted to their new environment. They started small businesses such as molding bricks from mud or hunting flying termites or mice and roasting them as a delicacy appreciated by their Angolan refugee neighbors. These entrepreneurs persevered and eventually raised considerable capital from those humble beginnings. Education, or at least the possession of a skill, often made the difference. So did letting go of their past and embracing their future.

Tom Albinson of the International Association for Refugees, one of our partner agencies, recently shared with me a graph showing the Continuum of Recovery along which displaced people travel. *See Figure 1.* The graph shows how any crisis hitting a people group creates sudden and rapid fall from normalcy. To avoid disaster, this fall must be slowed by emergency response. That's the role of UNHCR and its implementing partners.

Once the fall is contained and the people's basic survival is ensured, there is a need for recovery work that supports people in their return to normalcy. That's the role of There is Hope and similar developmental organizations, many of them local and faith-based.

To better understand the complimentary roles played by refugee relief organizations, read "There is Hope and UNHCR" on page 205.

Table 1: Continuum of Recovery

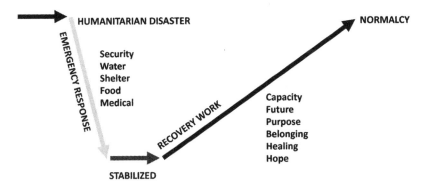

The sooner recovery work can begin, the fewer will be the numbers and the generations of people born and growing up in an unstable, insecure situation, surviving on emergency aid and nursing a victim mentality that will shape their identity and require a lot of work to undo.

I speak from experience. Thousands of second and third generation refugees have been born to my parents' generation, which fled Burundi in 1972. These stateless people find it very difficult to be accepted in their parents' country, having never lived there. Their best hope is resettlement, but this happens to less than 1 percent of the refugee population in any one year. What keeps people going is the hope that their children and grandchildren will become an integral part of their host community. That takes higher education or skills training.

In the next few paragraphs, I'll address the intentions and the efforts of the wonderful people who have made it their goal, either as a vocation or as a short-term volunteer, to come alongside the world's displaced populations.

First to Humanitarian Agencies: Relief aid is vitally important in the beginning of any crisis, but keeping people on relief for the long term handicaps their dignity and their ability to live on their own. Dependency is a destructive force that has crippled Africa since colonization.

During my 27 years in camps and settlements, I've admired Jesuit Refugee Services for their exclusive focus on building the capacity of refugees to identify and meet their own challenges.

Another common mistake agencies make, whether consciously or subconsciously, is planning great programs in the West and implementing them elsewhere. On too many occasions, such programs fail and the targeted group will share, after the fact, the doubts and concerns they had from the outset. More can be accomplished when the targeted group is involved early in the planning stage to identify their problems and to brainstorm possible solutions.

Next to Host Countries: I consider myself fortunate for having been born in a refugee settlement rather than a camp. Although life in Congo's Kenya-Tanganyika settlement was hard, we were not living on aid, and we could make a living for ourselves. We were subjected to discrimination by the locals, but we still had a sense of belonging to the village.

I highly recommend the joint strategy of UNHCR and the Zambian government, which gave land and equipment to displaced people living in Meheba Refugee Settlement and limited emergency aid to less than two years. This arrangement encouraged self-sufficiency from the onset.

Some host countries decline to provide extra land or integration for refugees, arguing that their territory is small and refugees would take over the economy. But overall, host countries do so much for refugees just by giving them a place to live in safety.

Now to Individuals Who Want to Help: I'm speaking here to volunteers, aid workers, churches, and other individuals. Every effort and intention to engage with the global refugee issue is admirable, and I encourage it. At the same time, I've noticed that fundraising for a vocational training center to address long-term refugee prospects does not attract nearly the level of response that fundraising for a program to feed orphans does. Likewise, a volunteer vacancy in the office of a local NGO is considerably more difficult to fill than opportunities for volunteers to *love on* refugee children for three weeks.

Be careful that, by coming to Africa as a volunteer, you are not primarily meeting your own need to feel accomplished and virtuous. Imagine a person stuck in a pit and you have two choices. You can either join her neighbors who are pulling the person out with a rope—or you can get into the pit with her, hand her a loaf of bread, take pictures for your Facebook page, and then leave. Consider a major mental shift away from pity and toward supporting the committed, long-term experts on the ground.

> *Read a "Westerner's Inside View" on page 207 to learn what working in an African refugee camp is really like.*

Many volunteers and short-term relief efforts want to do what they assume is needed rather than what would result in the most sustainable good. If you want to help, I encourage you to consider the following:

- Emergency response for short-term, urgent needs. But beware! If you give aid or emergency relief to those who are not in an emergency situation, you create dependency, which will cripple them and their children. Likewise, if you give a microloan to someone in need of emergency help, their business will collapse with no chance of repayment, because they will use the loan money for basic survival.

- Capacity building programs to aid recovery. Fund and volunteer for programs that aim to equip people who are already stable to earn a living for themselves, as a transition towards independence and to restore their dignity.

A word of caution: Expect problems in all interactions between the *haves* and the *have-nots*. Whether in our family, at work, or in the community, giving always comes at great personal investment. It can be rewarding when this sacrifice produces a positive outcome, but when our giving is misused or abused, we can feel hurt and develop resentment or a feeling of uselessness.

Personally, I am encouraged to keep giving without expecting those I help to make me feel good when I remember the words of Jesus who said, "Whatever you do for the vulnerable, you do for me." My responsibility is to give wisely; their responsibility is to receive wisely. Neither of us is responsible for the other's actions. The reward will come from above.

Finally to All Who Have Ever Been Displaced: I'm speaking here to former refugees and asylum seekers like me, as well as to people who have been internally displaced. KEEP THE CHAIN OF HOPE GOING!

> ***To all who have ever been displaced:***
> ***"Keep the chain of hope going!"***

The positive impact that people have had on our lives becomes more evident when the story does not end with us. Helping one person with a significant contribution, such as paying for their whole university education, may seem extravagant—even excessive. But if that person excels academically and professionally and goes on to support others who need a hand up, that investment will prove wise and the yield will be great.

If we have received such high-value and very personal help, we must understand that the giver was well aware of the difference that amount could have made in the lives of many. Yet they helped us, expecting that we will pass on to others their hope and support.

So many refugees remain emotionally stuck in their past, unable to grab the opportunities handed down to them. Their minds are numb to any other reality than the one they are in. As a teenager in Meheba Refugee Settlement, I remember crying whenever I went into the forest to collect firewood. I looked at the four corners of the camp as insurmountable walls and viewed the situation in my birth-country as utterly desperate and without hope. I spent so much time stressing over my reality that I developed stomach ulcers.

It took meeting a number of people in the community, especially at church, who spoke words of hope and shared stories of people who had overcome, for a light to go on inside me.

If you and I have come out of such situations, we have a unique ability to speak into the lives of those still trapped in the camps and emotionally in the past. In our newly found comfort, we must not close ourselves to them. Rather, we must realize that our own inner healing will be complete if we manage to stay connected to the reality from which we emerged. We'll do this by engaging with the refugee communities we

left behind and by affecting positive
change there.

    What I am suggesting is not easy.
Many people will request and expect
help from us. Surely we understand
their plight. I, myself, am constantly

*On page 211,
meet two former
refugees who are
"Giving Back."*

flooded with requests from people with whom I went to school or
church, or lived as a neighbor. I can only handle this situation by remind-
ing myself that I cannot help everyone, but I can make a difference by
helping one person at a time.

MY ROAD AHEAD

My wish is that there would be a global political desire to maintain peace
so that conflicts which arise are resolved amicably and promptly. My
heart sinks when I see the potential of Africa, based on the continent's
resources, but hear that the world still considers all fifty-four countries
to be "developing."

    Africa is making life easier and better for people in other parts of the
world as corrupt local leaders and their international allies siphon our
resources. From cocoa beans to diamonds, we have much wealth that
others refine and sell back to us. Yet, year after year our governments
go begging for budgetary aid to run our hospitals and schools and fix
our roads.

    Meanwhile, African presidents cling to their positions for dear life.
They often resort to modifying their country's constitutions so they can
be voted in again and again, as if their plans are so magnificent that they

> *To learn the family secret I uncovered while researching this book, read "The Blood Flowing in My Veins" on page 215.*

cannot possibly be implemented in two terms.

My dream is to one day hold a position of leadership that would give me a voice to make positive reforms in the political systems of my country and of the continent as a whole. This has been my dream since childhood, and after uncovering my full heritage while researching this book, I am even more convinced I could make a difference.

A VISION FOR THERE IS HOPE

Most African refugee camps are situated in remote areas where life isn't easy for the local population. When the locals see international and local NGOs flocking to their area to provide help to refugees, it usually creates resentment and animosity between the two communities.

There is Hope strives to bridge the gap between refugees and their neighbors by extending our programs to benefit local communities as well. With the rapid growth of the world's cities, refugees and locals living in remote areas will soon be on the move. The best way to help them succeed wherever they go is to offer them a movable capital. This capital is a skills set which is relevant to their local context but easy to carry with them when they relocate.

Another of my dreams for There is Hope is to establish a business arm with a manufacturing component that could fund needed services, respond to job creation, and generate funds to enhance what donors give for charity. This is not an effort to devalue the generosity of our contributors but rather a way to move in the direction of reducing complete donor dependency in our work with refugees.

Whatever the future holds for There is Hope, I pray our greatest budget item will always be the time we invest in our beneficiaries, whether the refugees of Dzaleka or their Malawian neighbors. After viewing a photo of There is Hope's community center constructed just outside Dzaleka Refugee Camp, a friend exclaimed, "It's in the middle of nowhere!"

> *There is Hope: Building a beacon of hope in the middle of nowhere.*

I kept thinking about her words. "That is exactly what There is Hope stands for," I concluded, "to build a beacon of hope in the middle of nowhere."

All of us at some point in our lives find ourselves stuck in the middle, whether emotionally, financially, or otherwise. In the middle of that emptiness, we need something or someone to inspire us—to propel us forward.

If only there could be a *somewhere* in the middle of every *nowhere*. The world would be a more hopeful place.

AUTHOR'S POSTSCRIPT

When I Look Back

Looking back on my life as a refugee, I see both the good and the bad circumstances working together for my benefit.

You may wonder why I consider the remembrance of often painful circumstances to be good. It is virtually impossible to appreciate difficulty while in its grip, but afterwards it is possible. In fact, difficulty can be as important as peace and comfort. Both work together to build one's character and appreciation of who God is.

Furthermore, although I have crossed over from refugee life, I am not through with difficult situations. Our recent experiences as parents of a disabled child underline that fact. But coming through this and earlier trials as a refugee, I realize that I have an important story to tell. I have been sharpened by past glories as well as past hurts, similar to the way both positive and negative charges work together to generate electricity.

This story expresses my gratitude

In my refugee past, thousands of people from different continents worked together on my behalf. Those who sent donations to charitable organizations such as UNHCR, Free Methodist Church, Lutheran World Federation, Red Cross, Jesuit Refugee Service, and other humanitarian organizations have contributed to my success without knowing me personally.

In my role as director of There is Hope, I have met some of the people who support this organization through their prayer, encouragement, provision of materials, and in many other ways. But many I do not know. This book is my attempt to reach out to all who have transformed my life. Because most of you are beyond my ability to meet and thank personally, I resolve to do good as long as I live, as an act of gratitude.

Many times in my early years, the circumstances of life tempted me to take shortcuts. I confess that, at times, I did. Yet, a strong inner voice often persuaded me to do right, to wait patiently for opportunity, and to resist the belief that I am defined by my circumstances.

As I look back, I see God orchestrating the opportunities and people who contributed to changing my life. Why God? Because I believe in him. Because my story is all the proof I need. Without a supernatural hand directing the course of my life, its random sequences could never have produced any good. Because with him, THERE IS HOPE.

23 DEEPER STORIES

For those who wish to further explore the historical events, the family life, and the refugee experiences described in Refugee for Life, these short stories will add perspective.

A Meeting of Survivors

On a Sunday morning in November of 2013 I attended a church in my family's hometown of Gitaza, Burundi. The mood was jubilant as the congregation praised God for his goodness and mercy.

That same day, in the afternoon, I sat with a dozen village elders in a residence just a few meters from the church. The mood of this second gathering was somber. Those assembled bore grim testimony to events occurring almost forty-two years before. In April of 1972 the blood of hundreds of family, friends, and neighbors had flowed freely into the rocky soil of this village on the eastern shore of Lake Tanganyika.

For the most part, the men and women assembled had been children or young adults in 1972. As the killings began, some fled Burundi for Congo (to the west) or Tanzania (to the east and south). Others remained and were spared by virtue of their age or gender—women and small children were usually not targeted. All recounted the killings as if they had happened yesterday. In 1972, I had not yet been born, so these were my elders. I have assigned fictitious names to the men and women who gave testimony on that Sunday afternoon, as they may still face recrimination.

A farmer named Emile, who grew up with my father Meshack, remembered him as a gentle and quiet man.

"When the killings started, the aim was to wipe away all educated Hutus and those who had money—like your father," said the man, confirming that the goal of the 1972 killings was to acquire the wealth and subvert the influence of the opposing tribe.

"Those who were lucky were able to cross the lake," said Emile. "Like your father, I fled to Congo." Not all of Emile's family left Burundi, however. "Those who stayed were killed," he added solemnly.

Throughout Burundi, local officials drew up lists of people to be killed, he recalled. Officials referred to people on these lists as *abamenja* meaning "rebels" in the Kirundi language. Emile identified the man who drew up these lists in the Muhuta District (where Gitaza is located) as Joseph Rudigi, the district administrator.

Several of the elders present this Sunday afternoon confirmed what I had heard earlier: Mr. Rudigi instructed members of a patriotic youth organization, the Jeunesses Révolutionnaires Rwagasore, to bring him the people on the lists. The JRR locked the *rebels* in a house not far from where we were meeting and proceeded to loot their prisoners' properties.

When Mr. Rudigi came to Gitaza, he would ask the JRR, "Do you have twenty or thirty in custody?" Then he ushered the prisoners down by the lake and killed them with knives under a mango tree, according to Emile.

*   *   *

My cousin Gustave picked up the story from there. "They didn't bury the killed people," he said. "They dug a hole to put all of them in—like animals." When the killings began, Gustave was in Kanyosha (now part of Bujumbura) with Dad, buying gas to resell. The two men returned to Gitaza and witnessed Mr. Rudigi stabbing people. Reportedly, over 20,000 people were killed in our district alone.

"How could the JRR round up so many people and lead them to their death?" I asked.

"At that time, the Burundian people were loyal to their leadership," Gustave replied. "If someone came with a letter sent by a leader, he could easily escort thirty people to their deaths."

Sometimes the victims were invited to attend conferences. When they arrived, they were surrounded and shot. Other times, Mr. Rudigi would go to the schools and tell the school administrators that a child's parents wanted him. As the child followed him away from the school, Mr. Rudigi would kill him. Gustave lost a brother that way.

Mr. Rudigi also traveled to other parts of the country to find and kill people on his list. One man at our Sunday afternoon meeting had a brother who taught high school in another district. He died at Mr. Rudigi's hands.

*   *   *

A man named Jean-Pierre spoke up next. "Some people on the lists eluded their captors by fleeing to the mountains," he said. "Mr. Rudigi sent people after them."

"Others escaped to Congo in industrial fishing boats holding about ten people each," he continued.[1]

Those who stayed in Burundi and did not die still suffered greatly, according to Celine, a woman who saw it all.

"The army and the JRR were shooting, and people were constantly running away from the shootings," she recalls. "Houses were burned and there was no support for the women whose husbands were killed or fled the country."

Fearing for their lives, older children fled the country, too. But smaller children were generally spared and stayed behind. They found life extremely difficult. Many of these children were not allowed to go back to school, and those who did were not permitted to attend after the sixth year of primary school. In addition, small Hutu children were taught in Kirundi only; no French instruction was provided, presumably to keep the tribe from producing future leaders.

*   *   *

Surprisingly, many of the JRR sent to bring *abamenja* to Rudigi were young Hutu men. They had joined the organization and rounded up members of their own tribe to be killed, in order to prove their loyalty and avoid capture themselves. But they did not escape either.

"After the Hutu JRR had done their work, Mr. Rudigi killed all

---

1   This was the route Dad took, fleeing first to the mountains, and then across Lake Tanganyika.

but one of them," stated Benoit, another man to speak that Sunday afternoon.

Benoit then informed me that Mr. Rudigi had suffered the same fate the very next day. Below is the account he gave:

About fifteen young Hutu men who had escaped to Congo returned to Burundi with plans to assassinate the district administrator. "If we do not kill him," they reportedly said, "he will finish our people." So, the young men ambushed Mr. Rudigi as he traveled from Bujumbura to Magara, at a place called Makombe.

On the Sunday following Mr. Rudigi's death, those who lived near the graveyard where he had been buried reported seeing smoke coming from his grave.

"Everyone who saw it would say his grave had caught fire," said Benoit, adding, "People wondered whether it was God's judgment, or at least they were consoled by such a thought." [2]

---

2   I obtained the quotes and facts reported in this story from a round-table discussion with men and women who lived through the 1972 killings.

Running for His Life

A prosperous businessman, my father, Meshack Surwavuba, possessed land, houses, and multiple means of generating an income in our home country of Burundi. That is, until the 1972 killings of Hutus with wealth or education forced him to flee to neighboring Congo.

For the first months of my family's existence in Congo, Dad worked at a variety of unpleasant jobs in exchange for food. Even after he established a trade in cattle and fish, my family lived as paupers compared to how they had lived in Burundi.

Those who claim that all refugees are migrants in search of economic gain have not seen and do not understand the complete mental, emotional, and physical devastation of being forced to leave or be killed.

Furthermore, the facts do not support the claim that refugees seek economic benefit in their flight. If that were true, then the overwhelming majority of the world's refugees would not be sheltered in the world's poorest nations. If that were true, refugees would not be restricted from working in their host countries. Or if they were allowed to work, they would not be restricted to menial jobs that few citizens of those countries will do.

If that were true, my father would have emerged from his exile a richer man. Instead, Dad spent a lifetime attempting unsuccessfully to regain the wealth he had possessed in Burundi.

To the Reader: That some refugees have become wealthy later in life does not negate the seriousness of the risk they faced before fleeing. Likewise, it is wrong to assume that because many present-day refugees come from developing nations, they must have been poor at home. Multiple layers exist, even in developing countries, and war is not a respecter of class.

Myth: Most refugees leave their country for economic reasons.

Truth: People who leave their country in pursuit of economic benefit are *migrants*, not refugees. By definition, refugees are people forced to flee their country due to war and/or persecution.

—*Tom Albinson, President,*
International Association for Refugees

Sharing Food with Ducks

In Kenya-Tanganyika where I grew up, ducks, chickens, and even goats roamed freely, along with dogs and cats. At mealtimes, people ate first and we fed the animals wandering the perimeter of our gatherings only after we had had enough.

Women and children ate in one circle, in the kitchen or out in the open. Men sat on chairs, further away. The women sat on small bits of brick or wood, while the children sat on the ground.

If we had meat or fish at a meal, the women would put a small piece of protein into the hand of each child. Gravy the protein was cooked in was left in the middle of the circle to share.

Ducks were the boldest of all the animals. They'd waddle around the circle, trying to grab protein from the hands of children not watching.

One day, a duck snatched my food. I got up with anger and kicked it like a ball. The duck hit the wall and died. I was in big trouble for killing family property. Adults shouted at me. "You should have let it go," they said. "We would have given you another piece."

That night we feasted on the duck, and ironically they gave me a big portion because it was thanks to me that we had meat to eat.[3]

---

3   A family of seven or eight would not finish a whole duck or chicken at one sitting. The bird would last a minimum of two meals.

Animosity toward Newcomers

When refugees from Burundi first populated Kenya-Tanganyika settlement in Congo, few Congolese lived nearby. Eventually, the Congolese moved closer and began to occupy lands not reserved for refugees. In general, our Congolese neighbors despised us Burundians and told us so whenever they had the opportunity.

Knowing our love for legumes, they would hurl insults like, "If you want to pacify a Burundian, just give him a pot of beans."

"This is not your land," the Congolese said to shame us. "You are only here because your own people rejected you." They further criticized our Burundian respect for leadership and intimated that we mostly Hutu refugees were spineless.

"If a Tutsi told you to open your month so they could spit in it, you would do it," said the Congolese. "If a Tutsi put the tip of his spear on your feet and told you not to break his spear—you wouldn't move."

As refugee children, we felt neglected and voiceless because our parents had fled from Burundi, and we had no hope of returning. Our differences with the Congolese sparked frequent fights among the students of my primary school, which served both refugees and locals. Girls and young children made noise while boys of both nationalities fought under the big mango tree on the way to Kenya village or under the sprawling eucalyptus on the road to Nundu village.

Soccer proved to be the ultimate contest between the local Congolese and the Burundian refugees. Win or lose, every match between us ended in a fight. If a Congolese fell in a contest with a refugee, he would yell, "I have been beaten by a Burundian!" Both his team and the spectators would run to his aid.

My brother Hari remembers one soccer match in particular. After the Burundians scored several goals, a Congolese player with nails imbedded in his shoes stepped on the bare foot of a Burundian. That sparked a heated contest in which the Burundians handily defeated the Congolese on and off the field. Until then, the locals had viewed refugees as weak and worthless; on that day, the Burundians united to fight the Congolese and won.

After that soccer match, they showed us greater respect, and we all got along better.

FRIENDS OF A DIFFERENT SORT

While some Congolese resented and teased Burundian refugees, the Kashindi family was different. These native Congolese treated us with respect. The family patriarch, Rondeur Kashindi, was an entrepreneur and became good friends with my father. He quickly recognized Dad's wisdom and experience in purchasing cattle.

While Dad's business was butchering cattle and selling the meat, Rondeur's business was building his herd. Whenever Dad saw a fine cow, he would tell Rondeur who would immediately go and buy it. In all things to do with livestock, Rondeur would follow Dad's advice.

As children, we emulated our fathers' friendship. The families kept their cattle together, and I remember my brothers and cousins herding cows from pasture to pasture with Rondeur's two sons, Kahindo and

Minyego. After finishing our chores, we would all go into the mango and banana groves and eat our fill.

More than two decades later, I still consider Kahindo and Minyego to be my brothers.

The Myth: Citizens of host countries welcome refugees with open arms.

The Truth: Developing countries host 86 percent of the world's refugees, often in the most impoverished areas. Sometimes citizens of host countries empathize with the plight of the refugees. Other times, tribal and religious differences result in animosity towards refugees. Some locals dislike the fact that refugees, out of their need to survive, willingly work for very little pay. Though any perceived harm is unintentional, locals claim this hurts the income and opportunities of the poorest in their communities.[1]

---

1   In recent years, humanitarian organizations have offered development assistance to host communities, in addition to caring for refugees.

UNHCR: Caring for Refugees

I lived in five refugee camps or settlements during my first twenty-seven years of life, beginning with Congo's Kenya-Tanganyika settlement. In all five locations, the United Nations (UN) or the Office of the United Nations High Commissioner for Refugees (UNHCR) played an important role in caring for me and my family.

The UN General Assembly created UNHCR in 1950 with a three-year mandate to help Europeans displaced by World War II.

Almost immediately, conflicts in other regions arose. In its own words, UNHCR stepped in to "lead and coordinate international action to protect refugees and resolve refugee problems worldwide." Operating as a nonpolitical entity, UNHCR works with host nations and a variety of non-governmental organizations (NGOs) to provide sustenance and security for refugees.

Over the years, UNHCR's mandate has been extended, and the refugee agency recently marked its 60th anniversary. The decolonization of Africa in the 1960s produced many refugee crises in which UNHCR played the crucial role of refugee advocate. Some crises, like the 1972 killings in Burundi, have required decades to address and resolve.

Again in its own words, UNHCR continues in this new century "to safeguard the rights and well-being of refugees" amid new conflicts on the African continent and around the globe.

While working diligently to meet the short-term needs of the

161

refugees, UNHCR endeavors to offer each refugee one of three durable (long-term) solutions to their plight.

1. Voluntary Repatriation – Returning to the refugee's country of origin in safety and with dignity when the crisis that drove them away has been resolved.
2. Local Integration – Incorporation of the refugee into the social, economic, and political life of their host country.
3. Resettlement – Emigration to a third country.

Regrettably, as my own story illustrates, repatriation can require years and is often complicated by issues like continuing violence, personal property disputes, the economic health of the country of origin, and many other factors beyond a refugee's control.

Likewise, local integration is often not available because of the social and economic burdens it places on the host country. In a recent year, over half the refugees for which UNHCR has taken responsibility resided in countries with a GDP per capita below US$5,000.

Finally, while the option for refugees to be resettled in industrialized countries is an important one, it affects a comparatively small number. The world resettled less than 1 percent of its refugee population last year.

Clearly these durable solutions fall short of being real options for the vast majority of refugees stuck in temporary spaces provided by UNHCR.

"This is not the fault of the agency or of the refugees," says Tom Albinson, president of the International Association for Refugees. "The world simply offers no alternatives."

Albinson mentions a fourth option which many displaced people choose: risking their lives by setting out on their own to reach the industrialized nations of the West in hopes of gaining asylum.

"This dangerous journey forces them to trust illegal human smuggling gangs to help them traverse deserts, jungles, and seas as they cross international borders in a desperate search for peace, safety, and a future," he states. "We tend to only hear of them when their boats sink or their bodies are found in the desert."

The Myth: Refugees eventually return to their countries of origin as soon as the crisis which caused them to flee is resolved.

The Truth: Returning usually ranks as the first preference of a refugee, but many live for decades outside their native country and some never return because 1) the crisis that caused them to flee has not ended, 2) their homes, lands, and jobs have been occupied by others, or 3) they have spent so long in exile that they no longer identify with their country of origin. The latter is particularly true of generations born to refugees after they have fled. The Office of the United Nations High Commissioner for Refugees works with other nations to find places for refugees when repatriation is not an option. However, there are far more people in need of resettlement than there are opportunities to resettle.

Hope Remains despite the Pain

While the assassination of President Ndadaye in October 1993 devastated Hutu refugees like my family, it sparked a genocide in which thousands of Tutsis perished.

Furious at Tutsi army leaders for extinguishing their hopes of majority rule, some Hutus blocked roads with trees, rounded up their Tutsi neighbors, and executed them. Hutus also died as army units clamped down, but the majority who lost their lives in the days immediately following the president's assassination was Tutsi.

An angry Hutu mob drove more than one hundred Tutsi students and teachers from the Kibimba Secondary School. The mob beat and hacked many of them to death before burning their bodies together with other Tutsis still living but roped together inside a gasoline station. According to an eye witness, the Hutu school administrator assisted in singling out and restraining the Tutsi students to be killed.

A Hutu rebel group attacked a Roman Catholic seminary at Buda, killing forty young seminarians ages fifteen to twenty. Entering their sleeping quarters at 5:30 a.m., the rebels ordered the young men to separate into two groups, so they could kill the Tutsis. The seminarians refused. Enraged at this, the rebels assaulted the group with rifles and guns, killing them all.

At age fifteen, Jean-Claude Nkundwa witnessed the execution of an off-duty soldier by a mob. When the mob began burning Tutsi houses (including his own) he ran outside and stared into their faces. "I saw people who I knew—who had shared wine with my family and whose children had shared milk with me," he recalls. "There had never been any conflict between us, but they had completely changed. They were angry, and they carried stones, spears, and machetes."

Terrified, Jean-Claude dashed through the crowd, evading stones and spears thrown at him and escaping into the countryside. But many of his family and friends died that day, as evidenced by a mass grave dug near his house.

Rosemarie Kadende-Kaiser, also a Tutsi, learned of the 1993 genocide while doing graduate work in the U.S. "With phone connections blocked the first couple of days," she said, "it scared me to think that I might be the only one left in my family."

Rosemarie eventually learned that her home had been looted and destroyed but that her immediate family had escaped. A female cousin and a handful of classmates survived the Kibimba Secondary School massacre by singing songs associated with the president's political party, leading the mob to believe they were Hutu. However Rosemarie's uncle Basile Samoya, a Catholic priest, died in the violence following the president's assassination. His parishioners chased and hacked him to death.

A dear friend lost nearly everyone in her immediate family during the tribal killings that swept a village in rural Burundi. Ten family members died, from newborn babies to the father in his 80s. "My friend and two brothers survived because they were not home at the time, but one of the brothers lost his wife and four children," says Rosemarie. She adds, "They are not the same people today, and because of their trauma, they never will be."

Despite these and other horrific accounts of the 1993 killings, stories of integrity and valor offer hope for national reconciliation. Rosemarie tells of her father, a Tutsi and a community elder, who in 1972 prevented a band of youth from killing innocent Hutus. "Because they respected my father as a leader, the youth let their victims go, and my father walked them home so they could survive," she explains.

By the same token, Rosemarie speaks highly of a Hutu headmaster who harbored the Tutsi students at a girls' school during the 1993 genocide. This headmaster called all Tutsi students to her and declared, "No one on my campus will die. You are staying with me, and I will protect you."

"My younger sister was one of those girls," adds Rosemarie.[4]

---

4   I obtained many of the quotes and facts reported in this story from personal interviews with Jean-Claude Nkundwa and Rosemarie Kadende-Kaiser.

Meheba Refugee Settlement

Zambia established Meheba Refugee Settlement in 1971 as a response to the tens of thousands of displaced people pouring over its borders during Angola's war for independence. The settlement continued to house Angolan refugees for almost forty years as warfare waxed and waned.

Located in the Northwestern Province of Zambia, Meheba has also served as a temporary home in recent years for thousands of Congolese and Rwandese fleeing conflicts in those countries. In addition, the settlement has played host to significant numbers of displaced people from Burundi, Somalia, and Uganda. Meheba's population peaked in 2001 at over 50,000 refugees and asylum seekers.

With a land area of 800 square kilometers (roughly equal to the size of Singapore) the Meheba settlement differs from a traditional refugee camp in that residents receive an allocation of farmland, tools, and encouragement to engage in subsistence agriculture. This worked well for Angolans with the natural inclination to farm and less well for Congolese who preferred other trades. One of Africa's oldest refugee communities, most children born in Meheba in recent years have lived only there.

Meheba Refugee Settlement functions as an agency of the Zambian Ministry of Home Affairs operated in cooperation with UNHCR. The settlement is divided into eight blocks (A-H) with side-roads one kilometer apart running perpendicular to a main thoroughfare dissecting the camp. Walking from one end of the camp to the other can take hours—even longer in bad weather.

The Master Mechanic

While visiting Meheba Refugee Settlement in Zambia, I met a man named Muchaila Chigambo. This sixty-five-year-old from Lubumbashi in D.R. Congo has been a displaced person since one of that nation's many wars forced him out in 2000.

Muchaila began looking for work in his profession as an auto mechanic soon after arriving at Meheba. Putting aside part of his earnings from each job, he began buying cars, trucks, and even minibuses that nobody wanted. As a mechanic, he knew exactly what parts he needed to replace to make these junkers reliable.

Repairing each of them, Muchaila hired drivers and put these vehicles on the road carrying passengers and cargo. Today, he owns a fleet of six cars, vans, and buses and is in the process of refurbishing more vehicles.

But here is the astonishing part. Muchaila is using part of his profits from his auto mechanic and transportation business to put his two sons through medical school.

I asked Muchaila what he'd do if he had to choose between going back to Congo or accepting an invitation to stay in Zambia. "I'd stay," he said.

Muchaila is still a refugee, but he is also a master mechanic who took the initiative to forge a new life in his country of refuge, despite the legal limitations placed on refugees living and working outside

UN camps. His story is not uncommon among refugees throughout Eastern Africa.[5]

A Myth—UN refugee camps primarily shelter uneducated or lazy people content with sponging off international aid organizations.

The Truth—Refugee populations contain the same mix of motivated and unmotivated human beings found in general populations. While the UN and partner non-governmental organizations (NGOs) make every effort to provide the basics for refugees, budgets often fall short and refugees themselves must play a part in their survival. Resilient, resourceful people reside in UN refugee camps, rich in talents to be shared with the world.

---

5   I obtained quotes and facts for this story from a personal interview with Muchaila Chigambo.

Lost beneath the Waves

Ten-year-old Anna, her mother, her older sister, and four of her sister's children boarded the boat for the night trip on Lake Tanganyika, the second largest freshwater lake in the world. Actually, the *boat* consisted of two wooden fishing boats lashed together. Normally, these boats would be occupied by four men fishing with nets. But tonight they would transport thirty-five men, women, and children, along with some of their belongings. The rowers pushed off from the mainland shore. Their destination: Congo's Ubwari Peninsula where they hoped to board motorized boats for the journey across the huge lake to relative safety in Tanzania.

It was the start of the 1996 Congolese War, and Burundian refugees living in the Kenya-Tanganyika settlement faced attack, arrest, and seizure of their properties. Some would die.

The journey on Lake Tanganyika had to be made at night to avoid gunfire from rebels along the shore. The first night proved uneventful. The water was calm. The boats pulled in to the shore at daybreak, and the refugees slept. Shoving off once again after dark, they prepared to spend another night on the lake.

Suddenly, a fierce wind arose and waves began to pound the travelers. One of two poles connecting the boats snapped in half and both boats capsized, dumping their human contents into the water. Several in the boat, including Anna's mother, could not swim and slipped quickly beneath the waves. The rest clung desperately to the over-turned boats.

Those holding onto the first boat decided to kick free of the second boat and propel it with their feet toward some lights in the distance. "Wait here and we'll come back for you," they said. Later, two women from the second boat decided to swim for shore using empty twenty-liter cans for flotation. One of these was my brother Josephat's wife, Cizanye. The rest, numbering seven and including Anna, held onto the second boat. At times, the waves would push them away from the boat, but they would always swim back. This happened again and again for three nights and two days.

One by one their numbers diminished. It happened according to a predictable pattern. The weakest would begin to hallucinate and say things unrelated to their present situation, like "I have some delicious food to eat back in Kenya. I think I will walk back there." Within a few minutes of the hallucination, that person would be swept away by the waves. With insufficient strength to swim back, they sank at last below the surface.

On the third day, only three remained: ten-year-old Anna, a pregnant woman, and my half-brother Sadock. Then Sadock began to talk crazy and let go of the boat. Anna swam to him and encouraged him to swim back, which he did. "You can make it," she told him. About that time the pregnant woman said to Anna, "Look, there is a boat in the distance."

"You are not seeing things, too, are you?" asked Anna, thinking the woman had begun to hallucinate. "I thought you and I would be strong enough to survive."

"Will I be the last one to die?" Anna cried in her heart to God.

"No," said the woman. "There really is a boat coming—see!" Anna looked and now she could see the boat slowly approaching. It was a family taking dried fish to market. At first they were hesitant about the voices coming from the overturned boat, thinking they were spirits of Lake Tanganyika. After satisfying themselves that these were real people in the water, the family pulled all three aboard and rowed them to shore. Here they found a friend of Anna's to help them recover. Eventually, the pregnant woman, Sadock, and Anna reached the peninsula where Anna's father waited. Knowing he would be devastated, she could not speak as she approached him. Out of their entire family, only his youngest daughter had survived. The two eventually found refuge in Tanzania.

Seventeen years had not diminished the memory or the pain of that awful experience. Telling her story to me in Tanzania's Nyarugusu Refugee Camp, Anna broke down in tears.

"It was the 15th of December in 1996, a day I will never forget," she said.

"I'm thankful to God that He kept my life," she added. "I didn't have strength to rescue myself."[6]

To the Reader: No one from the first boat or the two women who swam for the peninsula ever reached land. Besides my sister-in-law Cizanye, I lost my cousin's wife and their four children in the angry waters that night.

---

6   I obtained many of the quotes and facts for this story from a personal interview with Anna Ninkunze.

A Myth: Host countries offer refugees a safe haven for as long as they need to recover from physical and psychological distress and to rebuild their lives.

The Truth: Many countries generously offer displaced people refuge within their borders, but this is never a permanent guarantee. Refugees remain safe only as long as the political and economic condition of their host country remains stable. When their refuge is threatened, the journey of displaced people to a safer country can be fraught with danger.

A Refugee Advocate

News of unrest in a refugee camp may be met with the assumption that displaced people are ungrateful for the help that has been extended to them. Their participation in any demonstration is likely to be judged illegal by the court of public opinion. Little effort is made to draw a distinction between a minority of people in any population who like to cause trouble and those simply advocating for their rights.

The latter describes a man named Putois Ciband Chaboud.

Of Congolese nationality, Putois was a university student studying philosophy and preparing for religious life in 1998 when war forced him across the border into neighbouring Zambia. "They thought I was a soldier, so they locked me up in prison for one year," he states.

The Zambian government finally awarded Putois his status as a refugee and took him to Meheba Refugee Settlement in northwestern Zambia. There he lived until 2010, but not without ruffling a few feathers.

In 2000, Putois and others noticed non-refugees entering the settlement and bribing officials to give them ration cards. "One person might get food equivalent to 500 people and resell it," said Putois. They also observed non-refugees posing as refugees and offering bribes to the officials to put them at the head of the line for resettlement in the West. These two fraudulent dealings were particularly detestable to actual refugees. They threatened daily survival by depleting the food supply and their hope for a future by robbing them of a precious chance to emigrate.

So Putois decided to act. He wrote letter after letter to the Office of the United Nations High Commissioner of Refugees (UNHCR) and to the Zambian government protesting corruption at Meheba. His agitations did not go unnoticed. "I was arrested, taken to court, and beaten many times," he stated.

In 2009, UNHCR sent a delegation to investigate. At the conclusion of their investigation, they met with Putois and other protesters.

"Mr. James Lynch, UNHCR's highest officer in the region, acknowledged that there was indeed corruption," said Putois. Several high ranking staff members at Meheba Refugee Settlement were eventually replaced as a result.[7]

Unfortunately, Putois' refugee activism had gained him an odious reputation. He and twenty others were deported by the Zambian government in 2010.[8]

---

7   While Putois speaks for himself, the fact of corruption at Meheba and the subsequent replacement of leadership was confirmed in a conversation I had with the settlement's current refugee officer, Joseph Musonda.

8   I obtained many of the facts and quotes used in telling this story from a personal interview with Putois Ciband Chaboud.

Music Releases Pain, Recharges Hope

In the Congolese settlement where I was born, I sang in a children's choir and my brother Josaphat taught me chords on a guitar made from a used oil tin and wood and strings made of fishing lines.

In Tanzania's Nyarugusu Refugee Camp, I bought my first *tin* guitar and began to compose music. I was very troubled about my life, my future, and my country. Singing was the only thing that helped me deal with the pressure. I would take my home-made guitar and sing the songs I had written. Then, I would weep. After weeping, I felt lighter and free of stress.

Singing and dancing is probably not what first comes to mind when you think of a refugee camp. More likely, you imagine drudgery and hopelessness. Having lived as a refugee for twenty-seven years, I can tell you with some authority that music is very much a part of camp life.

Singing, playing music, and dancing, whether at life events or functions in or out of church, is the norm. When people sing and dance, they undress themselves of their burdens, enter an invisible ring, release the pain, and recharge their hope.

For this reason, There is Hope supports the arts as it works with various groups in Dzaleka Refugee Camp north of Malawi's capital city, Lilongwe. Dzaleka is home to people from five different African countries. Even where national or language barriers divide people in the same camp, music brings them together.

Making Congo Better

John Atanda, an educator and a refugee, wants to go home. Home is the territory of Fizi in South Kivu Province, Congo from which he fled the civil war in 1996. John lost all his possessions. He was captured and tortured by rebels but escaped with his wife.

John and his family have lived in Nyarugusu Refugee Camp north of Kigoma, Tanzania for the past seventeen years. I've known John for fourteen of those years. He taught me in secondary school.

From the moment he arrived in Tanzania with his wife Tosha Masoka and his first son, Eloge Ilunga, John's desire has been to one day return home. After seeking temporary shelter in Kigoma, the family moved to Nyarugusu on December 23, 1996.

Throughout his life as a refugee, John has endeavored to improve himself and the lives of those around him through education. He worked first in community health. Soon, because of his credentials as a teacher, John helped found the camp's first refugee school.

"We began by teaching under the trees," recalls John. "We didn't have a single book or blackboard to write on."

After two years, classes moved indoors when the United Nations International Children's Fund (UNICEF) began sponsoring primary school in Nyarugusu. "They constructed buildings and primary-age children went to school in the morning while secondary attended in the afternoon," explains John.

Teachers lived on donations from food allotted to the refugees and occasional sponsorships by aid organizations. Seventeen years later and now vice-administrator of a secondary school, John Atanda still earns only about US$25 a month. Of course, this is not nearly enough to support his immediate family (which now numbers seven) and nine orphans for whom he has responsibility back in Congo.

But John finds motivation in his passion for education and in his desire to help women, children, and disabled persons at Nyarugusu. In 2000, he founded an organization called *Centre d'Education et d'Action Aux Droits de l'Enfant et de la Femme* (CEADEF) to advocate for these underserved populations of the camp.

Born in a French-speaking nation, John also has a passion for learning English. His aim is not to resettle in an English-speaking country, but to nurture his fledgling CEADEF through association with like-minded organizations around the world. When he returns to the Democratic Republic of Congo—whenever that may be—John wants to bring a mature CEADEF with him.

"My long-term goal is to grow this organization so that someday it can be implemented in my home country," says the life-long educator.[9]

A Myth: Most refugees seek resettlement in the West.

The Truth: Most refugees long to return to their countries of origin. The Office of the United Nations High Commissioner for Refugees refers to this process as repatriation.

---

9   I obtained many of the quotes and facts reported in this story from a personal interview with John Atanda.

Unrest in Mtabila

Mtabila Refugee Camp was the most heavily populated camp in the Kigoma region of Tanzania, when I arrived there in 1998. Located atop a hill, Mtabila did not offer refugees lands to cultivate, as Meheba did. Though forested, the refugees had cut almost all the trees in the camp to build shelters or to burn as firewood.

The UN camp hosted more than 50,000 Burundian refugees at its peak. Some of Mtabila's Burundian residents had been there since the 1993 conflict. Others were Burundians who fled to Rwanda during the 1972 war but were forced, during the 1994 Rwanda genocide, to Congo and then to Tanzania. Still others, like me, had been born of Burundian parents who lived as refugees in Congo.

Another category of Burundians resided at the Mtabila camp: those who had been living abroad but chose to return to Burundi when President Ndadaye came to power. They were forced to flee again after his assassination. Finally, Mtabila hosted the exiled dignitaries of Ndadaye's government, including members of parliament, ministers, and governors. These diverse backgrounds proved to be an obstacle to harmony in the camp.

Attitudes toward the political situation in Burundi differed from one refugee to another. Everything that happened in Burundi also affected the camp and its residents, positively or negatively. For example, if a misunderstanding had existed between two Hutu rebel groups, that same misunderstanding would be played out in the camp among the supporters of the two quarreling parties.

With such an unstable atmosphere, I felt under threat of conflict and attack, even among my own people. For this and other reasons, I chose to continue my secondary school studies at Nyarugusu Refugee Camp instead of at Mtabila.

A Myth: Refugees find calm from their native country's political and tribal conflicts within the confines of UN sponsored camps.

The Truth: Political and tribal conflicts existing before a people group is displaced often transfer to their place of refuge, creating unrest and serious security issues within UN camps.

Refugee Deception

As you read my story, you've probably noticed a common practice in my journeys from camp to camp. Arriving at a border, I pretended to be whoever I needed to be in order to pass into the neighboring country.

Traveling into Malawi from Tanzania, for instance, I pretended to be a Tanzanian on a day-trip to visit friends in Malawi. My ability to speak several languages helped evade the immigration officials and get me whatever I thought I needed—in this case, a passage to Dzaleka Refugee Camp where I would feel more secure and have more educational opportunity.

This drove me to learn the languages and dialects of various places where I lived during my first twenty-seven years. Many times I impersonated a citizen of the country I was in simply to avoid the stigma of being a refugee. Whatever motives I had for what I did, it was definitely illegal in the eyes of the countries through which I traveled, and it was definitely deceptive.

Deception is a common practice among refugees and an unfortunate part of refugee life, even among those considered spiritual. I lived in five camps and settlements in four African countries, and in each of those countries I observed refugees practicing deceit in one form or another in order to survive. It is a sad fact that telling the truth will seldom change undesirable circumstances, so refugees tell what they referred to as *white* or *saving* lies.

The scarcity of opportunity for resettlement to developed nations often leads these displaced people to tell horror stories of war, to exaggerate the truth, or to make up a story that will move the heart of the listener. To be considered for resettlement, refugees must show they are insecure returning back home and insecure staying where they are. A few refugees have even been known to arrange for their houses to be burned to the ground in order to strengthen their case for resettlement.

Refugees sometimes claim their biological children belong to relatives who died, making them orphans and qualifying them for more food assistance. Since widows attract extra benefits, like food and plastic sheeting to cover their leaking grass roofs, some women claim their husbands have died or deserted them. Actually, their husbands live in a separate house and come home regularly to be with their family.

Let me set the record straight: I am not proud of my dishonesty, because it was wrong and does not portray who I am. However, because I lived in that culture for so many years, I do understand that refugees are conditioned to tell those in authority what they want to hear in order to survive.

They may also see telling a tall tale as what is needed in a corrupt system to obtain their fair share of what has been donated. Observing the theft of resources by the leadership of some camps, the refugee may reason, "If those distributing it have taken the best of what has been donated, why can't I have more?"

It is common knowledge that the population of Africa lives with a certain amount of corruption in everyday life, and the temptation for African refugees to deceive is made even worse by their desperation.

To the Reader: It may help you to comprehend the mind of an African refugee if you think of deceptive practices common in the West—like neglecting to report all income on your annual tax return, speeding, or taking supplies from your employer while rationalizing that the company has more than enough and will not feel the loss.

A Match Set Alight
by Florisa Magambi

I saw Innocent briefly in 2004, on a visit to Dzaleka Refugee Camp. He looked like anyone else there—a match in its matchbox. I recall nothing remarkable about him, apart from his hot pink windbreaker, which my *mzungu* eyes thought slightly odd for a man.

When I met Innocent again in 2006 and we spent time talking, I came away with a very different impression. From the smile on his face to the vivacity of his eyes, he immediately stood out. Like a match out of the matchbox and suddenly set alight, he had power, he had purpose, he was visible, and he was about to shine his light on others.

I believe Innocent has resilience and a sense of identity that few have, refugee or not. The freedom he acquired through education, a passport, and being accepted as a meaningful part of his host community simply unlocked his potential, which had previously been limited.

Others who escape refugee life might be resettled to the West, obtain citizenship, and even receive a university scholarship. Not all have the strength, however, to remain engaged with the life they leave behind and to use their pain so that others may find some relief. It's the same in our Western context: all of us have access to a range of opportunities, but not all use these opportunities to their full potential and for the benefit of others.

When I observe Dzaleka's refugees, I see a lot of buried potential. I desperately want it to burst out of the grave. It's a human tragedy that, were the next Beethoven or Picasso among the children born and living in a refugee camp, we would never know. They don't have the instruments, the coloring materials, or the access to be known to the outside world.

It has been a great privilege to offer a hand up to refugees in various small ways through There is Hope. It's a lot of pressure to choose the most deserving beneficiaries from an immense group of people. Lately, I have learned that we don't own people just because we help them. We all know this at a rational level, yet subconsciously we invest so much of our expectations in them that we hate to be disappointed. They will make mistakes after we've helped them. We must be very careful not to limit their freedom one more time by keeping them entangled in our help—never letting them go and always telling them what to do.

It has also been my joy to work alongside Innocent as he directs There is Hope. My husband may seem harsh at times, refusing to hand-hold our beneficiaries, but I know that he understands the value of freedom like few others.

To the Reader: Florisa has been working at There is Hope in a variety of roles over the years. Together, Florisa and I raise three sons: Jo and Sammy (twins) and their older brother Teo.

Children Waving at Airplanes

Soon after I received my first passport and officially exited the ranks of displaced people, a Christian organization invited me to facilitate a workshop in South Africa. They chose me to speak on organizing church response to migrants and refugees.

At age twenty-seven, that was the first time I flew on a plane, and it was an amazing experience. When I lived as a small boy in Kenya village on the shores of Lake Tanganyika, I never knew a black man could fly. I thought airplanes only carried *wazungu* (white people). If you were black and flew in an airplane, you must be a president or a minister.

The children in my village waved at every plane passing overhead. We believed that, if there were *wazungu* aboard the aircraft, they might look down and think "Oh, poor Africans . . ." and throw bread or even money to us below. So we waved at every aircraft, whether close to the ground or very far away. We just waved and tried to attract the attention of *wazungu*, but they never threw anything to us.

Years later, on the way to that South African conference, my mind wandered back to my childhood. I found myself thinking, "If I were flying over Kenya village right now, perhaps someone would wave at me."

Our Afro-European Merger

By mid-2008, when Florisa and the senior leaders of International Teams visited Malawi, I knew we were moving towards working together full-time and towards marriage. However, I did not have what I then referred to as "God's confirmation" that Florisa would be my future wife. I prayed and expected one day to hear his deep voice whispering in my ear. That day did not come, despite much fasting and praying.

Nevertheless, I felt my love toward Florisa growing, and I wondered what would happen when this Italian woman moved to Malawi to be a full-time employee of There is Hope. I did not want to marry the wrong woman and have to go through divorce, which had been a very painful part of my childhood. I also worried about people gossiping and assuming we were a couple because of the amount of time we spent together. I fretted about a couple of other things as well—our economic differences and our cultural differences.

Economic: In African culture, the husband is king over the household. I was at the same time excited and anxious about marrying a wife who had traveled and worked and who was articulate. Traditionally, marrying a woman with more money than her husband is unacceptable. My core fear was whether I would be respected. I assumed that a wife respects her husband only when he takes on the greatest responsibility—that is, to provide for his family. Though my girlfriend came from a different culture, I questioned whether she would continue to respect me if I didn't provide fully for the needs of our home.

Cultural: I was raised in a community where every adult contributed towards instilling good behavior in young people. Anyone had the right to discipline a child or teenager, without consulting the parents, whenever the child did something unacceptable. We Africans belong to the entire community. We aim to please everyone as much as possible; we withhold telling the truth if we think someone will be hurt. The side effect can be a shallow kind of friendship which lacks confidentiality because information is shared among many. As a result, the average African will have hundreds of "family members" and so called "friends." Yet, it is possible for that same person to have nobody to talk with about private and difficult issues.

On the other hand, Florisa grew up in a culture where people largely mind their own business—a culture where even parents do not have the right to impose their decisions on their children. That culture promotes few but high quality relationships, where transparency and trust are possible without fear of gossip. In her birth culture, you can do pretty much what you want without having to consider if people in the community will approve of it. The side effect is that people can become individualistic and insensitive to others.

It terrified me that Florisa might start sharing private information with people she perceived to be my close friends—people who would not be able to handle this information in confidence.

Though these differences scared me, I was encouraged by the way we handled our disagreements with respect and openness. The similarity of our vision for the future and our common passion to work among refugees supplied the framework for our day-to-day interaction.

To the Reader: When Florisa told her parents and shared her fears concerning our cultural and economic differences, her mum encouraged her that character is the most important thing in a man. I also told my siblings and extended family about my friendship with Florisa. Some expressed excitement about the prospective honor of having a white person in their family and thought that marrying into a white family would mean financial relief for the whole clan. Others expressed fear that I would move to Europe and no longer participate in our extended family's life.

Role of the Church in the Camp

After fleeing civil war in Congo as a seventeen-year-old, I spent a lonely year in Zambia's Meheba Refugee Settlement, not knowing if my family or anyone else I knew had survived. Even in those dark days, I drew comfort from the faith instilled in me as a boy and from belonging to a community of believers.

In 1997, the BBC World Service announced to refugees in Meheba the disheartening news that Congo's capital city, Kinshasa, had been captured by the rebels. Along with other Congolese/Burundian refugees, I experienced an overwhelming sense of loss and despair. I wondered if I would ever return to my country of birth, let alone to my family's beloved Burundi.

The following Sunday, my refugee church sang songs of surrender to God, with lyrics like "God knows all my fears. He sees everywhere. He is all-powerful."

Church played a vital role in my life. It presented another view of my situation as a refugee—that God was aware of my plight and was still able to bring hope and a way out.

Worship injected both hope and comfort at a very distressing time for me and my fellow refugees. If the church had not been there, we would have been totally hopeless and subject to misbehavior that characterizes those who feel life does not matter.

Human beings will do terrible things—abuse alcohol and drugs, rape, steal, kill, and even commit suicide—if they believe their only chance has been taken from them. Religious groups in refugee camps provide a moral compass and a sense that the members' faith community and its leadership will hold them accountable for their actions. What helped me most during my twenty-seven years as a refugee was a voice in my heart saying *"Don't give up. God has a plan for you."* I understood that Jesus and Mohammed had both lived as refugees and went through tough times, but they made it. This encouraged me to keep going, knowing that suffering does have an expiration date.

*   *   *

Now as I work in a refugee camp forty-five minutes northeast of Lilongwe, Malawi, we have seen the refugee church play a key role in providing accountability and psycho-social support to the women participating in our microloan program. The church also bridges the gap between refugees and local people by starting new congregations outside the camp and offering community development in under-resourced local villages. When people get married or have a funeral, the church or mosque acts as a family for many who have no relatives around them.

With dozens of houses of worship serving Dzaleka's residents, the church plays a pivotal role:

- It provides hope in the life of a troubled refugee.
- It provides counseling when conflict or misunderstanding erupts between refugees.
- It serves as a community hub with various activities such as worship services, choir rehearsals, prayer sessions, training, marriage ceremonies, and activities for children.

- It gives a platform to people to exercise public speaking, teaching, singing, and many other skills.
- It facilitates relationship among refugees of different nationalities, and it unites people of different social standing.[10]
- It responds first when death or sickness strikes the community.

Most importantly, the church delivers a message of hope and resilience essential to the long-term survival and recovery of refugees.

United Nations High Commissioner for Refugees, Antonio Guterres, whose organization looks after 51.2 million forcibly displaced people worldwide, has visited refugees and internally displaced people in dozens of countries since coming to UNHCR. On December 12, 2012, he stated: "Listening to their stories and witnessing their daily struggle in exile or displacement, I quickly understood that, for the vast majority of uprooted people, there are few things as powerful as their faith in helping them cope with fear, loss, separation, and destitution."

He continued, "Religion very often is key in enabling refugees to overcome their trauma, to make sense of their loss, and to rebuild their lives from nothing. Worship and religious traditions help uprooted people reconfirm their identity as individuals and as members of a community. Faith provides a form of personal and collective support among victims that is crucial for their ability to recover from conflict and flight. As such, faith contributes much more than many people think to the protection and well-being of refugees and other persons of concern to UNHCR and eventually to finding durable solutions."

---

10   Dzaleka hosts people from five major countries and thirteen distinct people groups.

Mwiza: The Big Impact of a Brief Life

I still wonder why some dreams come true and others don't.

My family struggled with polygamy and divorce. I wanted to be different and marry the right girl the first time. As a teenager and then as a young man, I met girls I really liked. But I didn't want to jump into marriage without first asking God, "Is this the one?"

Like many people, I believe God speaks to us in dreams. Several years before I married Florisa, I had a dream. The same dream occurred three times—at Nyarugusu, at Mtabila and again in Malawi, just after I left Dzaleka Refugee Camp to attend university.

In my dream, I saw a little girl in the arms of someone, while a voice said *"This is your daughter."* The little girl stared at me and smiled. Eager to study her face so I could know if it reflected a woman I had met or would meet in the future, I tried to approach her. But the person holding her withdrew further and further from me.

* * *

On August 13, 2010, Florisa gave birth to our first child, a daughter we named Mwiza Aurora. At birth, Mwiza did not look like the smiling little girl in my dream. She had a cleft lip and palate, and a severe brain malformation called Holoprosencephaly. In addition, her body produced neither the sleep hormone nor the hormone that regulates water absorption. This put her at constant risk of dehydration and made our nights virtually sleepless.

201

Due to the severity of her disabilities, doctors did not expect that Mwiza would learn to sit up or crawl. Her cleft palate prevented her from sucking. She also had dysphagia, meaning that she could not swallow properly, and extreme gastric reflux, which sent any milk or food we managed to get into her back up again.

After Mwiza's birth, I continued to dream. In one dream, I prepared to administer her medication. As I approached her crib, I discovered her sitting up on her own at age two. As I stood there in awe, time flashed forward and I saw Mwiza at age four, playing with another little girl. Again a flash and there was Mwiza at age 15, playing tennis. I ran up to her and held her. She spoke to me. *"I know you have suffered to raise me, but now I have grown,"* she said. *"Do not give up; Jesus is here to help you take care of me."*

*　　　*　　　*

Holding onto both dreams, I believed that God would heal our daughter and that I would one day see that beautiful smiling girl. Florisa and I looked for solutions on two fronts: medical science and divine healing.

For almost twenty months, we took our daughter to numerous specialists. Mwiza underwent three major operations, two at Great Ormond Street Children's Hospital in the United Kingdom to correct her cleft lip and palate, and one at Buzzi's Children's Hospital in Milan, Italy to introduce a permanent feeding tube straight to her stomach.

In addition, we took Mwiza to Spirit Word Church in South Africa, and I personally traveled to Lagos, Nigeria to visit the pastors of Synagogue, Church of All Nations, a church known to possess gifts of healing. While there, I observed people being healed and receiving prophecies, but I received neither.

In reality, Mwiza lived on seventeen different doses of various medicines per day and paid frequent visits to the hospital, until her veins had collapsed and could not tolerate either incoming IV fluids or having blood drawn.

In the spring of 2012, Mwiza contracted pneumonia. For five days she struggled to stay alive, even connected to breathing tubes at Kamuzu Central Hospital in Lilongwe.

One night she was particularly agitated. I caressed her until she fell asleep. As the night wore on, her breathing became progressively slower. The hospital staff tried their best to sustain life, but to no avail. I stood there absolutely helpless, watching the doctors working and our beautiful daughter fading along with my dreams.

Mwiza passed away early in the morning of April 17.

*   *   *

Why did one dream come to pass, but the other dream did not materialize as I expected?" To this day I cannot answer that question. Perhaps not everything in this life is meant to be understood.

This I do know. Our daughter's brief life opened our eyes to the generosity of those around us. Family and friends, as well as people we did not know, gave money, hospitality, time, their willingness to experience our pain with us, and much more. We don't know how we would have coped without them. Pain can be a very isolating experience, but being surrounded by love is a tool of great healing.

Mwiza's brief life also made us aware of disabled children near and far. We've grown closer to the community of disabled within Dzaleka Refugee Camp. There is Hope has since launched income-generating programs to utilize the talents and abilities of these parents, and to help them provide for their children. On Facebook, we've met parents the world over who have wrestled with their children's disabilities. What once was far from our minds is now near and dear to our hearts, as it is to God's heart.

As the impact Mwiza has had on us continues to play out in all we do, her story keeps unfolding.

There is Hope and UNHCR

At There is Hope, the desire of our hearts is to walk alongside residents of Dzaleka Refugee Camp and alongside the residents of vulnerable Malawian communities outside the camp.

Our approach has been to form relationships with the people we serve, rather than deciding and doing for them. We consciously avoid showing them the way or even telling them where they should be going. Instead, we walk with them in their joys and in their struggles, reasoning along the path and urging them to create their own solutions. When appropriate, we offer them a hand up if it would enable them to succeed on their own.

Allow me to make an important distinction between what UNHCR does and what There is Hope does. The Office of the United Nations High Commissioner for Refugees and its implementing partners (many of them internationally-based NGOs) do the necessary work of providing food and water, shelter, medical attention, early childhood education, and security for forcibly displaced people in Dzaleka and refugee camps worldwide, helping them to survive until a durable solution to their plight may be found.

There is Hope and a handful of NGOs like us focus instead on the long-term development of displaced people, empowering them to create their own solutions. To date, we have identified six key areas of effectiveness:

- Partnering with refugee churches to serve the community
- Arranging refugee scholarships for a university education
- Assisting, with training and microloans, those individuals and groups of refugees who wish to supplement their income
- Connecting with refugee prisoners by supplying basic needs in prison and aiding re-integration after release
- Fostering the artistic and creative talents of refugees
- Providing assessment and affordable orthotics and prosthetics to disabled refugees

In these and other areas yet to be realized, There is Hope seeks to compliment and collaborate with UNHCR and its partners, as we all work toward the well-being of the displaced people of Dzaleka and its neighbors.

I believe United Nations High Commissioner for Refugees, Antonio Guterres, cast a vision for us all in his opening remarks to the High Commissioner's Dialogue on Protection Challenges, December 12, 2012, in Geneva, Switzerland.

"I see faith-based organizations, and in particular local religious communities, as having great potential to more effectively contribute to the achievement of durable solutions."

A Westerner's Inside View

One purpose for writing this book has been to offer Western readers a means of looking behind the walls of a refugee camp and gaining a true picture of the people who live there.

In 2011, Americans Jacob and Jennifer Tornga became the first international couple to join the staff of There is Hope. Both grew up in Christian families and attended university after secondary school. Jake studied to be a pastor and Jenn studied to be a child psychologist. Their strong faith led this talented couple to volunteer for Africa with International Teams.

Raised in the West and having worked inside an African refugee camp, this couple is uniquely qualified to articulate how Western views of refugees differ from reality. I'll let them speak for themselves.

Jake: One thing I did not fully grasp before beginning to work in the Dzaleka camp is that being a refugee is not a choice. It is a situation forced on a person because he or she is from the wrong tribe, village, family, or religion. Likewise, a person cannot stop being a refugee simply by choosing to do so. Related to that, I thought of a refugee camp as a temporary holding facility. Actually, most refugee camps in sub-Saharan Africa are now permanent structures where multiple generations of people are born, live, and die without ever experiencing life on the outside. Similar to cattle, refugees are told where to go, where to live, where to get food, and so on. They have almost no choice in the matter, and they have limited opportunity to get out of this life because of international laws and their host nation's laws that govern them.

Before arriving in Malawi, I thought refugees had more freedom to seek employment, to get an education, and to go home if they wanted. But they are not legal citizens of their host country. They are there on refugee status, and whatever UNHCR and their host country determine is what they must do. They are legally required to obtain special permission if they wish to leave the refugee camp. So their freedom to move, their opportunity to work or to gain more education, and their freedom to make decisions are limited. This hopelessness is passed down through the generations, so that they do not even dream of the future. It would be quite reasonable for them to think: "What good is it to plan? My grandpa and my dad were refugees, and now I am a refugee. My children will probably be born in a refugee camp also."

Jenn: The biggest shift in my expectations had to do with what refugees needed from me. I imagined myself playing games, holding babies, clothing the naked, and feeding the refugees. In the West, these are common misconceptions of mission work. What is really needed, and what I am actually doing, is taking the knowledge I've been given about human behavior and sharing it with refugee educators who already know the language and the customs and understand the difficulties facing the children. That's because these educators grew up in the camp. My job today is different than I thought it would be when I arrived in Africa. The real need is for me to empower and lift up those who are teaching and empowering the refugee children.

Jake: When I came here, I did not understand the intensity of the receiver mentality in a refugee camp. Refugees tend to view everyone who is not a refugee as a means to get something to survive, as opposed to giving something. I didn't fully understand the psychological effect that being a refugee has on a human being. It forces refugees to relate to me in a way that will make me want to give them something when I hear their story.

Jenn: Generally speaking, a refugee will always say *yes* to any help that is offered, even if it is not what they need. They don't think beyond today, because of the situation they are in. Given the opportunity to get anything, they are going to say *yes*. Because of the oppressive circumstances that keep them confined, it is hard for refugees to plan their futures. This is why when There is Hope asks scholarship applicants "Where do you see yourself in ten years?" they are often unable to answer the question. Immediate survival is of greater concern than their prospects for the future.

Jake: Another thing we didn't expect was the negative perception of refugees by the local communities surrounding a refugee camp. Decisions to set up refugee camps are made on a national level, but many locals are mistrusting of refugees. It's not just that they ignore the refugees.

Jake and Jennifer: What we believed when we came, and what has actually proven to be true, is the general lack of development and opportunity, as well as a staggering level of poverty in places that host refugees. Those refugee camps we saw on TV or on YouTube before arriving in Africa do, in fact, present an accurate picture of what we've found in Africa.[11]

---

11   The information from this story came from personal interviews with Jacob and Jennifer Tornga.

Giving Back

It is one thing to pull yourself out of the misery of a refugee camp and start to piece your life together. It is quite another to choose to involve yourself in the lives of those who remain in those difficult circumstances. Thankfully some former refugees are doing just that. Meet two of them: Lwabanya Marx, a native of Congo, and Renovat Nzeyimana, native of Burundi.

* * *

Marx was born at Nundu Hospital, where I was born. He grew up in Congo's Fizi District where I also grew up. In 1996, I fled the advancing rebel forces. Marx fled with his family. Both of our families lost everything and eventually took refuge in Tanzania. But Marx and I did not meet until he tutored me in mathematics as I prepared for my secondary school examinations in 2002. He had just finished secondary school in bio-chemistry and was very good at math.

Presented an opportunity to study medicine later that year, Marx left the Nyarugusu camp and risked an unstable political situation to attend university at Bukavu, D.R. Congo. He earned his medical doctorate in 2009. Marx currently practices at a Free Methodist university hospital in Bujumbura, Burundi, and teaches at the university as well.

Having "made it" on the outside, Dr. Lwabanya remains active in the Nyarugusu Refugee Camp where the rest of his family still lives. He continues to encourage its youth through an NGO he co-founded in his last year of medical school. "Twice a year I share my life experience at youth retreats involving eighty boys and girls," he states. "My talk centers on my experience with God as the key to my success."

In addition to other conferences, seminars, and workshops at which he speaks, Marx coaches twenty-six refugee youth on leadership and entrepreneurship.

Marx, who is no longer a refugee, also volunteers with D.R. Congo's Tumaini Sports Academy. Its motto: Stop revenge—score for peace!

"Refugee life has taught me to learn from the positive aspects of my circumstances and that the best life is one dedicated to serving others," he states.

*   *   *

Renovat Nzeyimana is a Burundian whose family fled to Rwanda in 1972 for the same reasons my family fled to Congo. The massacres of 1994 forced Renovat, who grew up in Rwanda, to flee again—this time to Tanzania. Like me, Renovat later fled to Dzaleka Refugee Camp in Malawi in search of a more stable place to look for a way out.

In November 2005, UNHCR Malawi selected Renovat, his wife and three children for resettlement in Norway.

After learning the Norwegian language and completing his bachelor's degree in nursing, this former refugee is reaching back into Dzaleka Refugee Camp to help others make a new start in life. He currently supports the University Scholarship Program of There is Hope. He has re-visited Dzaleka more than once since resettling in Norway, and has taken steps to raise awareness of the camp in his adopted country. His most recent project is to organize an annual bike ride in the town of Elverum, Norway, to fund university scholarships for Dzaleka refugees.

Renovat believes that higher education is the number one tool for alleviating the poverty and hopelessness that refugees often face in a developing world. He himself was given a chance to study nursing while a refugee, and he wants to give the same opportunity to those he left behind.

"I feel it is my responsibility to try to do all I can to make a difference in the lives of refugees in Malawi by supporting them so they can get higher education," says the former refugee.[12]

---

12   Dr. Lwabanya's story was gleaned from personal interviews with the physician. Sources of Mr. Nzeyimana's story include a personal letter he sent to UNHCR in Lilongwe, Malawi and a newsletter published by There is Hope.

The Blood Flowing in My Veins

Conducting research for *Refugee for Life* has given me an opportunity to learn more about my family tree than I ever imagined.

In Burundi, we do not have a family name that we take from our father. Rather, each person is given two first names. In addition, many births, marriages, and deaths are not recorded at local government offices. Where archives once provided a record, many have been burned or misplaced during war. All these make it very hard to trace one's forefathers.

Growing up, I knew my father belonged to the Abahanza clan, which is the most influential clan in the Hutu tribe. The Abahanza are well-known in Burundian history for their wisdom and presence in the king's palace. I had no knowledge of my mum's clan. I did not even know the name of her father, my maternal grandfather.

In 2010, I interviewed some of my relatives to piece together any information they might have concerning my grandparents and other family history. My sister Miriam told me that, when we moved back to Burundi in 1993 and President Ndadaye was assassinated, she had been arrested by a group of Hutus forming a militia to resist the army's attacks. They accused her of being a Tutsi and wanted to kill her. Only by saying the name of our dad, who was well-known in the area, was she recognized as Hutu and released. That experience stuck in her mind, and she later questioned our maternal aunt but got no answers.

As Miriam and I talked in 2010, I recalled something similar from

215

my childhood. Growing up in Congo, people in our village would tell me that my hair was soft like a Tutsi's. I took that as an insult. After all, our family had been forced from Burundi in 1972 by Tutsi persecution.

I asked Miriam to approach our now elderly maternal aunt one more time, explaining that I was writing a memoir and needed to know more about my mum's lineage. What I heard on July 30, 2010 totally shocked me.

According to this aunt, my maternal grandfather was a Tutsi from the Abenengwe clan, and one of his names was Kanyoni. His mum, whose tribe we don't know, divorced after giving birth to Kanyoni and married a Hutu. This Hutu step-father had to keep his step-son's tribe a secret, or Kanyoni might have been mistreated. As an adult, Kanyoni married a local Hutu woman and from that marriage my mum was born.

I did not know what to make of this revelation. Part of me was a people that I had been conditioned to dislike. I felt betrayed by my parents, although I understood that if people knew Mum was Tutsi, we would have risked being stigmatized and isolated. At the same time, I felt I personally should have been told. None of my siblings knew this either—not until 2010.

Nowadays, I am simply amazed to think that ethnic lines that have hated and battled each other for years could reside in my DNA. How I wish I could someday play a part in bringing peace to my country. I know it must be possible, because the blood of the Hutu and the Tutsi flows in my veins, without conflict and distinction.

I am both.

BIBLIOGRAPHY

BBC. "Burundi Profile." May 21, 2013. accessed March 28, 2014. http://www.bbc.com/news/world-africa-13085064.

Chrétien, Jean-Pierrre. "The Great Lakes of Africa: Two Thousand Years of History." New York: Zone Books, 2003.

Committee on Migration. "Safeguarding Protection and Durable Solutions for Asylum Seekers and Refugees in Southern Africa." United States Conference of Catholic Bishops. September 2013. accessed June 4, 2014. http://www.usccb.org/about/migration-policy/fact-finding-mission-reports/upload/Safeguarding-Protection-and-Durable-Solutions.pdf.

Cultural Orientation Resource Center. "The 1972 Burundians–COR Refugee Backgrounder No. 2." March 2007. accessed April 11, 2014. www.culturalorientation.net.

Guterres, Antonio. "High Commissioner's Dialogue on Protection Challenges, Theme: Faith and Protection." Opening remarks at Palais des Nations. Geneva, Switzerland: UNHCR, December 12, 2012.

Heritage Foundation (The). "The 2014 Index of Economic Freedom." 2014. accessed March 29, 2014. http://www.heritage.org/index/country/burundi.

International Association for Refugees. "IAFR's Unique Role on the Highway." accessed January 16, 2015. http://iafr.org/news-2/250-iafr-s-unique-role-on-the-highway.

International Association for Refugees. "10 Myths Concerning Refugees." accessed September 10, 2014. http://iafr.org/downloads/handouts/10myths/10%20Common%20Myths%20Concerning%20Refugees.pdf

Lemarchand, René. "Case Study: The Burundi Killings of 1972." June 2008. accessed March 06, 2014. http://www.massviolence.org/Article?id_article=138.

Quinn, Frederick. "African Saints: Saints, Martyrs, and Holy People from the Continent of Africa." New York: Crossroads Publishing Company, 2002.

There is Hope. "A New Partner in Norway." There is Hope Newsletter, March 2014: 2.

Tuhabonye, Gilbert. "This Voice in My Heart: A Runner's Memoir of Genocide, Faith, and Forgiveness." New York: Armstad, 2007.

United Nations. "General Assembly Resolution 428 (v)." New York: UN, December 14, 1950.

United Nations. "International Commission of Inquiry for Burundi: Final Report." New York: United Nations Security Council, 1996.

United Nations High Commissioner for Refugees. "Displacement: The New 21st Century Challenge." UNHCR Global Trends 2012. Geneva, Switzerland: UNHCR, 2013.

United Nations High Commissioner for Refugees. "History of UNHCR." n.d. accessed April 25, 2014. http://www.unhcr.org/pages/49c3646cbc.html.

Uvin, Peter. "Life After Violence: A People's story in Burundi." London: Zed Books, 2009.

Veroff, Julie. "Justice Administration in Meheba Refugee Settlement: Refugeee Perceptions, Preference, and Strategic Decisions." MPhil thesis, Oxford University, St. Anthony's College, May 2009.

World Bank. "Burundi Data." 2013. accessed March 11, 2015. http://data.worldbank.org/country/burundi.

There is Hope – The organization founded by Innocent Magambi, author of Refuge for Life. The vision of There is Hope is to see refugees, asylum seekers and vulnerable people in the host community rise above difficult circumstances by fully utilizing their potential, thus being self-sufficient and making a positive contribution to society. For the latest on this Malawi-based NGO, visit www.thereishopemalawi.org/.

International Association for Refugees – Publisher of Refugee for Life. This international Christian organisation is dedicated to mobilizing the church to seek the welfare of forcibly displaced people by meeting them on their journey, generating hope and helping them rebuild their lives. Learn more about IAFR and the Refugee Highway by visiting http://iafr.org.

To order additional copies of Refugee for Life,

visit www.refugeeforlife.com.